THE
LITTLE
BOOK
OF
CORNWALL

THE
LITTLE
BOOK
OF
CORNWALL

JOHN VAN DER KISTE

The
History
Press

First published 2013
The History Press
The Mill, Brimscombe Port
Stroud, Gloucestershire, GL5 2QG
www.thehistorypress.co.uk

Reprinted 2017

British Library Cataloguing in Publication Data.
A catalogue record for this book is available from the British
Library.

ISBN 978 0 7524 8095 4

Typesetting and origination by The History Press
Printed and bound by TJ International Ltd, Padstow.

CONTENTS

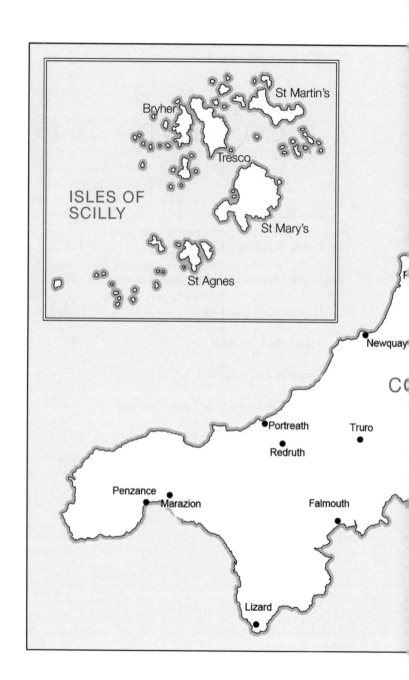

ISLES OF
SCILLY

St Martin's

Bryher

Tresco

St Mary's

St Agnes

Newquay

CC

Portreath

Truro

Redruth

Penzance
Marazion

Falmouth

Lizard

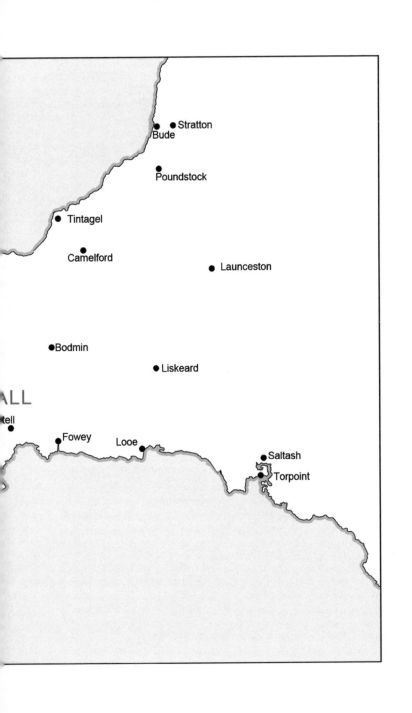

INTRODUCTION

Cornwall has always been on my doorstep and I have been a regular visitor to the county, whether going to explore and walk on Bodmin Moor, shop in Falmouth or Truro, or go to concerts at the late lamented Cornwall Coliseum. My happiest memory of the county, though, is of my wife Kim and I spending a delightful time in the Bude and Tintagel area shortly after we became engaged, and fittingly we started our honeymoon at Jamaica Inn and the Eden Project later that year. It goes without saying that I found it a tremendous pleasure and enjoyable challenge to compile this book. I could not have done so, however, without trawling through a variety of sources including books, pamphlets, old newspapers and journals, websites and, last but not least, my admittedly less than perfect memory. Thanks go to Kim, who read through the draft manuscript and recommended several improvements, to my old friend Miles Tredinnick, who was brought up in Cornwall and made several excellent suggestions, and as ever my editors at The History Press, Michelle Tilling and Richard Leatherdale, for their help in seeing the book through to publication.

1

ROYAL & POLITICAL CORNWALL

THE ROYAL DUCHY

The Duchy of Cornwall is an aggregation of estates vested in the eldest son of the sovereign or, in the absence of a son, lying dormant in the crown. Apart from the interregnum during the commonwealth after the execution of Charles I, the Duchy has existed since 1337 when it was created by Edward III for his eldest son Edward, 'the Black Prince'. According to a translation of the Great Charter of that year, the king's son was 'Duke of Cornwall and heir to the Kingdom of England'.

Before this date there were Earls of Cornwall, the first being Robert of Mortain, the half-brother of William the Conqueror, and after the king, at that time the largest landowner in England. Early in the twelfth century Reginald, one of the illegitimate sons of Henry I, assumed the title of earl, but after Stephen ascended the throne in 1135 he brought an army into Cornwall and awarded the title to Count Alan of Brittany. When Henry II came to the throne in 1154 he confirmed Reginald as earl. Others who were made earl in subsequent years included Richard of Cornwall, also called King of the Romans, brother of Henry III; Henry's son Edmund; Edward II's notorious 'favourite', Piers Gaveston; and after his murder, Edward's second son, John of Eltham.

Queen Victoria and Prince Albert made two cruises around the coast of the West Country and visited Mount Edgcumbe together in the 1840s. Tremayne Quay near Helford was built for a visit by the queen, but unfortunately she did not come because it was raining.

Queen Victoria's eldest son the Prince of Wales (and of course Duke of Cornwall), later King Edward VII, was present at the consecration ceremony for Truro Cathedral (see p. 132) in November 1887.

LEGENDARY CORNISH MONARCHS

According to the twelfth-century historian Geoffrey of Monmouth, writing in *Historia Regum Britanniae* (*History of the Kings of Britain*) in about 1135–8, *King Arthur*, a hero of the late fifth and early sixth century, was said to have been conceived at Tintagel. Uther Pendragon, a fifth-century King of Britain, went to war against Gorlois, King of Cornwall, to capture his wife Igraine with whom he had fallen in love. Merlin the wizard changed Uther's appearance so that he resembled Gorlois and enabled him to enter Tintagel, where he slept with Igraine – and Arthur was born as a result. However, despite claims made elsewhere to the contrary, Monmouth does not suggest that Arthur was born in the town or had any further connection with the area.

Mark of Cornwall, also early sixth century, was mentioned in Arthurian legend as the uncle of Tristan and husband of Iseult, who had an adulterous affair with Tristan. He was a contemporary of Salomon, another Cornish warrior prince.

Salomon of Cornwall was a contemporary figure of whom nothing else appears to be known. Some of these figures, who may or may not be purely legendary, were probably only rulers over very small localised areas of the county. Ricatus, who ruled in the tenth century, is one whose name is known only from inscriptions on surviving carved stone memorial crosses.

Dungarth, also known variously as Donyarth, Dumnorth, Dumgarth, or Doniert, was said to have been drowned in 875 in the River Fowey, and is commemorated on an inscription on King Doniert's Stone, a ninth-century cross shaft which stands in St Cleer parish.

Cadoc, or *Condor*, was said by the fifteenth-century historian William of Worcester to be a survivor of the Cornish royal line and descendant of Dungarth at the time of the Norman Conquest in 1066, and appointed 1st Earl of Cornwall by William the Conqueror. In turn he was believed to have been an ancestor of Thomas Flamank, the Bodmin lawyer executed in 1497 (see p. 150).

Teudar, who may have been a contemporary of King Arthur, was a notorious heathen said to be responsible for the martyrdom of St Gwinear and possibly other Christians who were later sanctified.

CORNISH NOBILITY

Barons Edgcumbe, later Earls of Mount Edgcumbe

Sir Piers Edgcumbe of Cotehele (1477–1539) acquired the Mount Edgcumbe estate through marriage in the early sixteenth century. One of his descendants, Richard Edgcumbe (1680–1758), Paymaster-General of Ireland and Chancellor of the Duchy of Lancaster, was created Baron Edgcumbe in 1742. On his death the title passed to his eldest son, another Richard (1716–61), Lord Lieutenant of Cornwall, and in turn to his younger brother George (1720–95), an Admiral and former

Treasurer of the Household. In 1781 George was created *Viscount Mount Edgcumbe and Valletort*, and in 1789 1st Earl of Mount Edgcumbe. The 8th Earl, Robert Charles Edgcumbe (1939–), succeeded in 1982, and the heir apparent to the earldom uses the courtesy title of Viscount Valletort.

St Aubyn Baronets, Barons St Levan

There have been two baronetcies created for members of the St Aubyn family. *The St Aubyn Baronetcy, of Clowance,* was created in 1671 for John St Aubyn (1645–87). All five baronets were named John, all became members of parliament, and the title became extinct on the death of the 5th Baronet in 1839.

The St Aubyn Baronetcy, of St Michael's Mount, was created in 1866 for Edward St Aubyn (1799–1872), the illegitimate son of Sir John St Aubyn, 5th Baronet of Clowance (1758–1839), on whose death the baronetcy of Clowance had become extinct. Sir Edward's son John, who succeeded him on his death, was created 1st Baron St Levan in 1887. The 4th Baron, John Francis Arthur St Aubyn (1919–), succeeded in 1978.

Earls of Godolphin

Earl of Godolphin was a title created in 1706 for Sidney Godolphin, 1st Baron Godolphin (1645–1712), Lord High Treasurer who was also created Viscount Rialton. He had been created baron in 1684. On his death the titles passed to his only child Francis (1688–1766). Francis married Henrietta, 2nd Duchess of Marlborough, but their only son, William Godolphin, predeceased his parents and died without issue in 1731. The 2nd Earl was created Baron Godolphin of Helston in 1735, with remainder, in default of male issue of his own, to the male issue of his deceased uncle Henry Godolphin, Dean of St Paul's. On his death the Godolphin earldom, the Rialton viscounty, and the Godolphin barony of 1684 became extinct; but the Godolphin barony of 1735 passed to his cousin Francis (1707–85), becoming extinct on his death. There was a third creation, as Baron Godolphin, of Farnham Royal, Buckinghamshire in 1832, which became extinct in 1964. The ancestral seat of the family in Cornwall was Godolphin House, near Helston.

CORNISH POLITICS

Since the early nineteenth century, the Liberals (now the Liberal Democrats) have not infrequently held the majority of parliamentary seats in Cornwall, with the Liberal Unionists or Conservatives in second place and Labour only winning one seat in General Elections between 1945 and 1966, and again in 1997 and 2001, when the party performed particularly well nationally. In the elections of 1906, January 1910, 1923 and 1929, all five county seats were won by the Liberals, although in 1950, 1951, 1955 and 1959 they failed to win even one, with the Conservatives taking four and Labour the remaining one. In 2005 all seats went to the Liberal Democrats. For the subsequent election in 2010, an alteration in constituency boundaries resulted in the county being divided into six seats instead of five, with the Liberal Democrats and Conservatives each winning three.

Bodmin holds the records for the smallest parliamentary majorities in the county. In the January 1910 election, Cecil Alfred Grenfell (Liberal) retained the seat with a majority of 50, but after he stood down Sir Reginald Pole-Carew (Liberal Unionist) won it at the subsequent General Election of December 1910 with a similarly narrow majority of 41. In February 1974 Robert Hicks (Conservative) lost by only nine votes to Paul Tyler (Liberal), but regained it at the next General Election seven months later with a margin of 665. Tyler went on to represent North Cornwall as a Liberal Democrat from 1987 until he stood down in 2001.

NOTABLE POLITICIANS AND CORNISH CONNECTIONS

Sir John Eliot (1592–1632), MP for his birthplace of St Germans from 1614, was an outspoken critic of King Charles I and his policies. He often spoke in the House of Commons against what he regarded as illegal taxation and insufficient enforcement of laws against Roman Catholics, was imprisoned on three separate occasions and died of consumption while in captivity in the Tower of London.

Leonard Courtney, later Baron Courtney of Penwith (1832–1918), Liberal MP for Liskeard from 1876, was for a time a member of Gladstone's administration, but helped to defeat the Home Rule for Ireland Bill in 1885. He later became a Liberal Unionist, but distanced himself from his colleagues after regular disagreements with other members and the leadership on policies which led to the Boer War, and left parliament in 1900.

Tom Horabin (1896–1956), Liberal and then Labour MP for North Cornwall from 1939 to 1950, became Liberal Chief Whip in 1945. He resigned from the party a year later as he believed they were becoming almost indistinguishable in their policies from the Conservatives, and took the Labour whip, but stood down from parliament three years later before a General Election in which he would almost certainly have been heavily defeated.

David Mudd (1933–), Conservative MP for Falmouth and Camborne from 1970 to 1992, was a well-known newspaper and local TV journalist before being elected to parliament, and the author of several titles on the county's history. A frequent rebel against party policies where he considered they did not benefit Cornish people or industry, he ended his career as an Independent Conservative about a year before standing down.

David Penhaligon (1944–86), Liberal MP for Truro from 1974 to 1986, served a term as Liberal Party President. Much-respected and admired by members and voters from all parties, he was regarded as a potential party leader and would probably have been chosen thus had it not been for his untimely death in a road accident.

Sebastian Coe (1956–), Conservative MP for Falmouth and Camborne from 1992 to 1997, had already enjoyed a successful career as an athlete before entering politics (see p. 172).

PRIME MINISTERS AND CORNWALL

At least five prime ministers have had some association with the county.

Arthur Wellesley, Duke of Wellington (1769–1852), remembered as the victorious commander at the Battle of Waterloo in 1815, and who subsequently became Tory prime minister from 1828 to 1830 and again briefly in 1834, is buried in a tomb at St Paul's Cathedral made from pink granite taken from the quarry at Luxulyan.

Sir Anthony Eden, later Lord Avon (1897–1977), Conservative prime minister from 1955 to 1957, spent some time convalescing in the county in December 1957 after a period of ill health which had led to his resignation from office. He and his wife rented Morval House near Looe for a short period, spending Christmas there prior to returning to London.

Harold Wilson, later Baron Wilson of Rievaulx (1916–95), Labour Prime Minister from 1964 to 1970 and again from 1974 to 1976, was Yorkshire born and bred, and sat for constituencies in Lancashire, but evidently had a soft spot for Cornwall. He joined the Labour Party at Liskeard during the Second World War, and his father Herbert lived for some time in his latter years at Biscovey. During his time in parliament Harold had holiday homes successively at Perranporth and the Isles of Scilly. Although he died in London, he was laid to rest in the grounds of St Mary's Church, Isles of Scilly.

Margaret Thatcher, later Baroness Thatcher (1925–2013), Conservative prime minister from 1979 to 1990, also spent regular holidays in Cornwall, particularly in the Constantine Bay area, during her years of office. In May 1983 she made the first public appearance of her second General Election campaign as party leader, according to a correspondent from *The Times*, by 'fondling a newly dead lobster in Cornwall' on the north coast.

David Cameron (1966–), Conservative prime minister from 2010 until 2016, was on holiday with his wife Samantha and their family in Cornwall during August 2010 while she was expecting their fourth child. The baby, a daughter, was born at Royal Cornwall Hospital, Truro, and named Florence Rose Endellion, the last after the village of St Endellion.

CORNISH ROTTEN BOROUGHS

From medieval times, Bodmin, Helston, Launceston, Liskeard, Lostwithiel and Truro had all been continuously represented in parliament. Fifteen further boroughs were added between 1553 and 1584. At the time of the Great Reform Act in 1832, Cornwall had twenty boroughs which between them elected forty members of parliament, in addition to two county members. Another borough, Grampound, had also elected two MPs until 1821, when it was disenfranchised by Act of Parliament because of widespread bribery, its voters claiming that they received 300 guineas each for their votes. Until then, the county therefore returned forty-four MPs, only one fewer than the whole of Scotland. Rotten boroughs were communities too small to justify separate representation, many also being pocket boroughs, controlled by a patron effectively able to nominate members unopposed.

Rotten boroughs abolished in 1832

Bossiney	Fowey	St Germans
Callington	Lostwithiel	Saltash
Camelford	Mitchell	Tregony
East Looe	Newport	West Looe

Boroughs retaining the right to elect members in 1832

Bodmin   Penryn, renamed Penryn and Falmouth
Helston   St Ives
Launceston   Truro
Liskeard

CORNISH NATIONALIST PARTIES

Mebyon Kernow (MK), meaning 'Sons of Cornwall', is a left-of-centre political party leading a campaign for self-government of the county through the establishment of a legislative assembly. It was founded by Helena Charles, a cultural activist and poet, in January 1951. She led the party for the first four years, and in 1953 she won the St Day seat on Camborne-Redruth Urban District Council with 77.6 per cent of the vote, under the slogan 'A fair deal for the Cornish'. Andrew George, Liberal Democrat MP for St Ives since 1997, was formerly a member of MK and in 2005 he became the first Cornish MP to swear his oath of allegiance to the queen in Cornish. The party is represented on Cornwall County Council, and again in 2005 became the largest political group on Camborne town council after a by-election, though it has yet to win its first seat at Westminster or in the European Parliament.

The Cornish National Party (CNP), which also campaigns for Cornish independence, was founded in 1975 by historian James Whetter, a former MK member who had stood twice for Westminster under his old party's colours. It ceased to exist in 2005 but reformed four years later.

CORNWALL'S STATUS

Cornwall's legal right to its own parliament has existed for several centuries. This was confirmed and strengthened by the Charter of Pardon in 1508, which added to its rights that of veto over acts, statutes, and laws passed by the Westminster government. These were granted in perpetuity and cannot be lawfully rescinded. Cornwall's right to its own sovereign parliament and the powers it possesses under the Charter of Pardon, were confirmed as valid in British law in 1977 by the then Lord Chancellor, Lord Elwyn-Jones.

In British law no officer or agent of the Crown, which includes both Westminster and the Anglican Church, can legally set foot upon Cornish soil without the express and joint permissions of the Duke of Cornwall and Cornwall's Stannary Parliament. In the Cornish Foreshore Case, an arbitration case held between 1854 and 1858 to resolve a formal dispute between the British Crown and the Duchy of Cornwall over the ownership of the foreshore of the county of Cornwall, officers of the Duchy successfully argued that it enjoyed many of the rights and prerogatives of a county palatine and that, while the Duke of Cornwall was not granted royal jurisdiction, he was considered to be a quasi-sovereign lord within the Duchy of Cornwall. This was interpreted as meaning that the duke, not the British monarch, was in fact the head of state.

Until the mid-sixteenth century, most maps showed Cornwall as a separate territory from England. At his coronation in 1509, Henry VIII listed England and Cornwall separately in the list of his realms which formed part of his address. Cornwall was not a party to the Act of Union, which united the kingdoms of England and Scotland to form Great Britain in 1707.

2

ARTISTS, ARCHITECTS, MUSICIANS & ACTORS

CORNISH PAINTERS, BOTH NATIVE AND VISITING

Thomas Luny (1759–1837), born near Mevagissey, although he spent most of his working life first in London and then in Devon, was a noted painter of seascapes, ships and naval engagements.

John Opie (1761–1807), born at Trevellas, St Agnes, was much admired for his historical pictures including *The Murder of Rizzio*, and portraits of members of the royal family, Samuel Johnson and others; sometimes known as 'the 'English Rembrandt' or 'the Cornish Caravaggio'.

J.M.W. Turner (1775–1851) travelled extensively around the south-west coast in 1811, and painted several pictures of scenes in Cornwall, including *Land's End, Cornwall, Looking out to Sea*; *St Mawes at the Pilchard Season* and *Entrance to Fowey Harbour*.

James Whistler (1834–1903) and Walter Sickert (1860–1942) both visited St Ives and the surrounding area in 1884, where they painted several coastal scenes.

THE NEWLYN SCHOOL

The Newlyn School comprised a colony of artists who worked in and around the town between about 1880 and the early twentieth century. Although they had not been born or raised in Cornwall, they were

attracted by the low cost of living in the county, the availability of inexpensive models and the long hours of daylight and natural light. Many were also inspired by the fishermen and their working lives at sea, as well as everyday life in the harbour and local villages. Prominent among them were Stanhope Forbes (1857–1947) and his wife Elizabeth (1859–1912), Samuel John Lamorna Birch (1869–1955), Henry Scott Tuke (1858–1929), Norman Garstin (1847–1926), Frank Bramley (1857–1915), Walter Langley (1852–1922) and Dame Laura Knight (1877–1970).

THE ST IVES SCHOOL

St Ives became a popular nucleus for artists after Bernard Leach (1887–1979) and Shoji Hamada set up a pottery there in 1920, and after Ben Nicholson (1894–1982) and Christopher Wood (1901–30) visited the town where they were impressed by the work of the primitive painter Alfred Wallis (1855–1942). As they decided to stay there, it was largely due to them that the port gradually developed as an artists' colony. Nicolson and his then wife Barbara Hepworth (1903–75) settled there shortly after the outbreak of the Second World War, establishing an outpost for more avant-garde artists, and were joined by the Russian sculptor Naum Gabo (1890–1977). A new, younger generation of artists settled here after the war, among them Peter Lanyon (1918–64), John Wells, Roger Hilton, Terry Frost (1915–2003), Bryan Wynter (1915–75), Denis Mitchell (1912–93) and Alan Lowndes (1921–78).

CORNISH ARCHITECTS

James Piers St Aubyn (1815–95) was renowned as a major builder and restorer of churches in Cornwall and Devon, and his restoration of St Michael's Mount is generally considered his greatest achievement. His major disappointment was a failure to secure the commission for building Truro Cathedral by one vote.

Richard Coad (1825–1900), born in Liskeard, worked extensively on Lanhydrock House and helped to rebuild it after it was damaged by fire in 1881, and was also Clerk of Works on the Albert Memorial, London.

Edmund Sedding (1836–68), spent much of his career at Penzance where he died, having built and restored churches at Gwithian, Wendron, Newlyn, Altarnun and St Stephens by Launceston, as well as being church organist and publisher of books of Christmas carols.

Silvanus Trevail (1851–1903), born at Luxulyan, Cornwall's most renowned architect of the Victorian age, designed the Headland Hotel, Newquay; Carbis Bay Hotel and restored a church at Temple.

Geoffrey Bazeley (1906–89), born in Penzance, was known for his Modernist architecture. He built Tregannick House, near Penzance, as well as other major buildings in the town, St Austell and Hayle.

MUSICIANS, SINGERS, COMPOSERS AND OTHERS WITH CORNISH ASSOCIATIONS

W.S. Gilbert (1836–1911) and *Arthur Sullivan* (1844–1900) wrote two of their operettas with a Cornish theme, *The Pirates of Penzance* (first performed 1879), and *Ruddigore* (1887), the latter being set in the fictional Cornish town of Rederring.

Richard J. Jose (1862–1941), born in Lanner but emigrated to America during his youth, was a countertenor who made several records during the early gramophone era.

George Lloyd (1913–98), born in St Ives, was composer of twelve symphonies, four piano concertos, and a Requiem in memory of Diana, Princess of Wales.

Moura Lympany (1916–2005), born in Saltash, was an internationally renowned concert pianist.

Dudley Savage (1920–2008), born in Gulval, organist and broadcaster, was best remembered as the main presenter of and performer on *As Prescribed*, a BBC radio request programme for housebound and hospitalised listeners.

Brenda Wootton (1928–94) was born in London but brought up in Newlyn, and thereafter was based in the county. Unofficially known as the 'voice of Cornwall', she was much respected as a folk singer in Cornish and Breton, a mainstay of local folk clubs, and later a radio presenter.

Derek Holman (1931–), born in Illogan, was a choral conductor, organist and composer.

Sheila Tracy (1934–2014), born in Helston, was a jazz musician who later also pursued careers as a radio presenter and author, mainly of books about jazz.

Benjamin Luxon (1937–), born in Redruth, is a baritone singer who specialises mainly in singing opera, but also early and contemporary song. After being afflicted by severe deafness he turned to giving masterclasses as well as becoming a narrator and poetry reader.

Alan Opie (1945–), born in Redruth, has been a baritone opera singer with several different British companies.

CORNISH POP AND ROCK STARS

Roger Taylor (1949–), drummer, moved to Truro during his childhood and was brought up there. He formed his first band The Reaction, who played gigs throughout Cornwall in the mid-1960s, and with whom he played drums and sang, leaving them to form Smile, who often played in Cornwall and London from 1968 onwards. During 1970 they changed their name to Queen, and their performance at Truro City Hall on 27 June that year is regarded as the first ever Queen gig, though they had been booked as Smile and still retained the name in advertising for a while as it had become so well-known. During the next year or so they also played gigs at Penzance, Hayle and St Agnes.

Ralph McTell (1944–) and *Michael Chapman* (1941–), singer-songwriters and guitarists, both came to the county, where they regularly (and independently) played the local folk club circuit in about 1966/7, shortly before signing their first record contracts.

Andy Mackay (1946–), born in Lostwithiel, was saxophonist and oboeist with Roxy Music.

Mick Fleetwood (1947–), born in Redruth, was drummer with Fleetwood Mac from their foundation in 1967, and one of only two constant members in a long-lived group who were renowned for their regular changes in personnel.

Al Hodge (1951–2006), born in Bodmin, guitarist, session musician and composer, was a member of Cornish psychedelic rock band The Onyx from 1965 to 1970, and co-writer of the Meat Loaf/John Parr 1986 hit 'Rock 'n' Roll Mercenaries'.

Tim Smit (1954–), founder of the Eden Project (p. 83), was for a while a songwriter, producer and arranger for acts including Barry Manilow and the Nolan Sisters before, in his words, 'deciding to do a Captain Oates and leave'.

Bruce Foxton (1955–), bass guitarist with The Jam and Stiff Little Fingers, had holiday homes in Polperro and Fowey, which he sold after his wife's death.

Tori Amos (1963–), singer-songwriter, pianist and composer, settled in Cornwall where she converted her barn into Martian Engineering Studios.

Aphex Twin, real name Richard James (1971–), electronic musician and composer, grew up and began his career in Cornwall.

Alex Parks (1984–), born in Mount Hawke, was a singer whose career was launched by winning the BBC's *Fame Academy* in 2003.

MUSIC TRIVIA

Blondie shot the video for their 1982 single 'Island of Lost Souls' at St Mary's Gardens, Tresco, Isles of Scilly.

Echo and the Bunnymen held a photoshoot for the picture used on the cover of their 1984 album *Ocean Rain* in Carnglaze Caverns.

Acts including Steeleye Span, Oasis, Supergrass, Muse, The Verve and Razorlight have recorded albums at Sawmills Studio, Golant, Fowey.

MUSIC VENUES

Carnglaze Caverns, Liskeard
Cornwall Coliseum, St Austell, formerly Cornish Riviera Club, closed late 1990s
Eden Sessions, Eden Project, Bodelva (annual one-day live music and comedy)
Falmouth Arts Centre
Hall for Cornwall, Truro
Princess Pavilion, Falmouth

CORNISH FOLK SONGS

'An Awhesyth', Cornish for 'The Lark', was one of the traditional county songs thought to date back to the eighteenth century, collected from an octogenarian pub owner by the Devon musicologist and author the Revd Sabine Baring-Gould and published in *Songs and Ballads of the West* (1889). 'Bro Goth agan Tasow' ('Old Land of our Fathers'), regarded as one of the county's anthems, is sung to the same tune as the Welsh and Breton national anthems, 'Hen Wlad Fy Nhadau' and 'Bro Gozh ma Zadou'.

'Cadgwith Anthem', also known as 'Robbers' Retreat', is an old drinking song of uncertain origin. The name of Cadgwith does not appear in the words. It became especially popular in 1975 after a largely unaccompanied version was recorded by Steeleye Span on their most successful album, *All Around My Hat*.

'Camborne Hill' celebrates the historic steam engine ride of Richard Trevithick up Camborne Hill on Christmas Eve 1801, although the tune is said to be based on that of a seventeenth-century protest song 'Levellers and Diggers', or 'The Diggers' Song'. It is often sung at Cornish rugby matches away and other gatherings. In 2001 survivors of the 9/11 attack recalled Rick Rescorla (see p. 157) singing it to keep morale high as he was evacuating employees from Morgan Stanley from the World Trade Center office shortly before it collapsed.

'Come, All Ye Jolly Tinner Boys' was probably written in about 1807, when the continuing success of Napoleon Bonaparte in invading other European territories was seen as a major threat to the tin trade at home. One of its lines, 'Why forty thousand Cornish boys shall know the reason why' may have inspired Hawker's 'The Song of the Western Men' (see p. 28).

'Delkiow Sivy' ('Strawberry Leaves') is an old traditional song, revived in 1975 by Brenda Wootton, who sang it as a duet with Robert Bartlett on her album *Starry Gazey Pie*.

'The First Nowell', a traditional classical carol believed to date back to the eighteenth century, is of Cornish origin. It was first published in *Carols Ancient and Modern* (1823).

'Hail to the Homeland', regarded as an unofficial Cornish anthem, was composed by Kenneth Pelmear (music) and Pearce Gilbert (lyrics).

'Lamorna', identified by sheet music in the British Library from 1910, taking its title from the village of the same name, is a song about the courtship of a man and a woman, who turns out to be his wife. A reference to Albert Square in the words has led to suggestions that it refers to Manchester, although this has not diminished its popularity, especially around Cornwall. It has been recorded by Brenda Wootton and the Yetties among others.

'Little Eyes', thought to have been introduced to the county as 'Honey Honey', recorded in the 1950s by American group the Deep River Boys, adapted by Camborne band the Joy Boys, became a local favourite and has remained popular in the Camborne area ever since.

'The Song of the Western Men', also known as 'Trelawney', regarded as a Cornish anthem, was written in about 1824 by the Revd Mr Hawker (see p. 183), about Sir Jonathan Trelawney, the Pelynt-born Bishop of Bristol, one of seven bishops imprisoned by James II in 1687. He based it on the old Cornish proverb 'And shall Trelawny die? Here's twenty thousand Cornish men will know the reason why,' although the refrain from 'Come, All Ye Jolly Tinner Boys' was probably also part of his inspiration. His words are a little inaccurate, in that the march on London to which he refers only reached as far as Bristol, before Trelawny was acquitted by a jury in London and released.

'Sweet Nightingale', also known as 'Down in Those Valleys Below', is probably seventeenth-century in origin.

'The White Rose' has long been a favourite with Cornish male voice choirs and is a regular choice for funerals.

THE DAVEY AND COLEMAN FAMILIES

The contemporary Cornish Celtic music scene owes much to both families. In the 1970s, Merv Davey was responsible for collecting many of the music and dances being played at the time by Cornish traditional musicians. Towards the end of the decade, he formed the group Bucca with brothers Andy, Kyt and Neil. In 1980 they became the first outfit to release a professional recording of traditional Cornish Celtic music, *An Tol an Pedn an Telynor* ('The Hole in the Harper's Head'). They had long been a musical family, and their mother had formerly been with local outfit the Goonhavern Banjo Band. When Bucca disbanded, Kyt went on to form another band, Anao, who released an album *Stones* in 1994. Towards the end of the decade Neil and Kyt joined forces with Hilary Coleman, Jen Dyer and Bec Applebee to form Dalla, who proclaimed themselves 'the first supergroup in Cornish Celtic music'. Within eleven years they had released four albums, *A Richer Vein, More Salt, Rooz* and *Cribbar*.

ACTORS, PERFORMERS, BROADCASTERS AND IMPRESARIOS

Samuel Foote (1721–77), probably born in Truro, was a dramatist and theatre manager who ran the Haymarket and later New Haymarket Theatres.

Mary Ann Davenport (1759–1843), born in Launceston, starred regularly in productions at Covent Garden and Haymarket Theatre between 1790 and 1830.

Robert Newton (1905–56), educated at Lamorna, was an actor who died in the United States but had his ashes later scattered in Mount's Bay.

Kenneth Kendall (1924–2012), TV presenter and journalist, brought up in Falmouth.

Robert Shaw (1927–78), lived and educated in Truro, was a film and TV actor and writer.

Rodney Bewes (1937–), TV actor noted for his comedy roles, especially in *The Likely* Lads and its sequel *Whatever Happened to the Likely Lads?*, lived in Cornwall for some years.

John Nettles (1943–), born in St Austell, Royal Shakespearean actor known for stage and TV roles, most famously leading roles in *Bergerac* and *Midsomer Murders.*

John Rhys Davies (1944–), and *Nigel Terry* (1945–2015), were film and stage actors, both educated at Truro.

Jeff Rowe ('Jethro') (1948–), born in St Buryan, is a comic known equally for appearances in the county and on TV.

Jenny Agutter (1952–), film actress who owns a second home at The Lizard.

Rory McGrath (1956–), born in Redruth, comedian and actor.

Kristin Scott Thomas (1960–), born in Redruth, best known for her roles in *Four Weddings and a Funeral* and *Gosford Park.*

Philip Schofield (1962–), broadcaster and TV personality, grew up at Newquay.

Thandie Newton (1972–), actress, grew up in Penzance.

THEATRES

Minack Theatre, Porthcurno
Sterts Theatre, Liskeard
Little Theatre, Padstow
Acorn Arts Centre, Penzance
Penlee Open Air Theatre, Penzance
Miracle Theatre Company, Redruth
Keay Theatre, St Austell
Kidz R Us, St Ives
Bedlam Theatre Company, Truro
Kneehigh Theatre Trust, Truro
Redannick Theatre, Truro

FILMS

The following feature films were shot partly on location in Cornwall.

The Manxman (1929), directed by Alfred Hitchcock, starring Carl Brisson, Malcolm Keen – Polperro, various sites in north Cornwall

The Mystery of the Marie Celeste (1935), directed by Denison Clift, starring Bela Lugosi, Shirley Grey – Falmouth

Yellow Sands (1938), directed by Herbert Brenon, starring Marie Tempest, Belle Chrystall – Sennen Cove

Jamaica Inn (1939), directed by Alfred Hitchcock, starring Charles Laughton, Maureen O'Hara – Bolventor

The Thief of Baghdad (1940), directed by Michael Powell, starring Conrad Veidt, Sabu – Gunwalloe

Ghost Train (1941), directed by Walter Forde, starring Arthur Askey, Richard Murdoch – Liskeard station

Next of Kin (1942), directed by Thorold Dickinson, starring Mervyn Johns, Nova Pilbeam – Mevagissey

Love Story (1944), directed by Leslie Arliss, starring Margaret Lockwood, Stewart Granger – Minack Theatre

Johnny Frenchman (1945), directed by Charles Frend, starring Tom Walls, Patricia Roc – Mevagissey

Miranda (1948), directed by Ken Annakin, starring Glynis Johns, Googie Withers – Carlyon Bay, Polperro, Looe

Scott of the Antarctic (1948), directed by Charles Frend, starring John Mills, Diana Churchill – Falmouth Docks

Treasure Island (1950), directed by Byron Haskin, starring Bobby Driscoll, Robert Newton – Carrick Roads, River Fal, River Helford, Falmouth

Never Let Me Go (1953), directed by Denzil Daves, starring Clark Gable, Gee Tierney – Mullion Harbour, Newquay, Mevagissey

Knights of the Round Table (1953), directed by Richard Thorpe, starring Robert Taylor, Ava Gardner – Tintagel

Night of the Eagle (1962), directed by Sidney Hayers, starring Peter Wyngarde, Janet Blair – Porthcurno Beach, Cape Cornwall

Crooks in Cloisters (1963), directed by Jeremy Summers, starring Ronald Fraser, Barbara Windsor – St Mawes

Straw Dogs (1971), directed by Sam Peckinpah, starring Dustin Hoffman, Susan George – St Buryan, Lamorna

Malachi's Cove (1974), directed by Henry Herbert, starring Donald Pleasence, Veronica Quilligan – Trebarwith Strand

The Eagle has Landed (1976), directed by John Sturgess, starring Michael Caine, Donald Sutherland – Newquay, Charlestown

Dracula (1979), directed by John Badham, starring Frank Langella, Laurence Olivier – Tintagel, St Michael's Mount

When the Whales Came (1989), directed by Chris Rees, starring Paul Scofield, David Threlfall – Bryher, Isles of Scilly

The Witches (1990), directed by Nicolas Roeg, starring Jasen Fisher, Anjelica Huston – Headland Hotel, Newquay

The Three Musketeers (1993), directed by Stephen Herek, starring Charlie Sheen, Kiefer Sutherland – Charlestown, Boconnoc, Lanhydrock, Pentire, Pelynt, Lostwithiel

Blue Juice (1995), directed by Carl Prechezer, starring Sean Pertwee, Catherine Zeta Jones – Newquay, St Ives, Mousehole, St Agnes, Godrevy

Twelfth Night (1996), directed by Trevor Nunn, starring Imogen Stubbs, Steven Mackintosh – Trebarwith Strand

Moll Flanders (1996), directed by Pen Densham, starring Robin Wright, Morgan Freeman – Falmouth, Charlestown

Oscar and Lucinda (1997), directed by Gillian Armstrong, starring Ralph Fiennes, Cate Blanchett – Boscastle, Port Isaac, Bossiney

Swept From the Sea (1997), directed by Beeban Kidron, starring Vincent Perez, Rachel Weisz – Crackington Haven, Bodmin

Mansfield Park (1999), directed by Patricia Rozema, starring Frances O'Connor, Harold Pinter – Charlestown

Saving Grace (2000), directed by Nigel Cole, starring Brenda Blethyn, Craig Ferguson – Port Isaac, Boscastle, Trebarwith Strand

Die Another Day (2002), directed by Lee Tamahori, starring Pierce Brosnan, Halle Berry – Holywell Bay, Newquay, Eden Project

Johnny English (2003), directed by Peter Howitt, starring Rowan Atkinson, Ben Miller – St Michael's Mount

Ladies in Lavender (2004), directed by Charles Dance, starring Judi Dench, Maggie Smith – Cadgwith, Helston, St Ives, Prussia Cove

Cold and Dark (2005), directed by Andrew Goth, starring Luke Goss, Kevin Howarth – St Agnes

Alice in Wonderland (2010), directed by Tim Burton, starring Johnny Depp, Mia Wasikowska – Antony House, Torpoint, Charlestown Harbour

TELEVISION

The following television films, series or episodes were shot partly on location in Cornwall. Inevitably the books of Daphne Du Maurier, Winston Graham, Rosamunde Pilcher and W.J. Burley, all set in the county, feature strongly on this list.

Magical Mystery Tour (1967), starring The Beatles – Newquay, Bodmin

The Onedin Line (1971–80), starring Peter Gilmore, Anne Stallybrass – Charlestown, Mousehole, Turnaware Point

Poldark (1975–7), starring Robin Ellis, Angharad Rees – general

The Goodies: Bunfight at the OK Tea Rooms (1975), starring Tim Brooke-Taylor, Graeme Garden, Bill Oddie – St Just

Penmarric (1979), starring Annabel Leventon, Peter Blake – general

The Camomile Lawn (1991) starring Jennifer Ehle, Tara Fitzgerald – Veryan, Portloe Harbour

Wycliffe (1993–8), starring Jack Shepherd, Jimmy Yuill, Helen Masters – general

Rebecca (1997), starring Charles Dance, Emilia Fox – Charlestown

A Respectable Trade (1998), starring Jenny Agutter, Richard Briers – Charlestown

Frenchman's Creek (1998), starring Tara Fitzgerald – Charlestown, Helston, Padstow, St Clement

Coming Home (1998), starring Emily Mortimer, Peter O'Toole – general

The Shell Seekers (1998), starring Angela Lansbury and Patricia Hodge – Land's End, Lamorna Cove, Marazion

Nancherrow (1999), starring Susan Hampshire, Patrick Macnee – Chapel Porth, Wheal Cotes, Newquay

Doc Martin (2004–), starring Martin Clunes – Port Isaac

Wild West (2002–4), starring Dawn French and Catherine Tate – Portloe

3

LITERATURE & LEARNING

CORNISH AUTHORS, BY BIRTH AND ASSOCIATION

Maria Branwell (1783–1821), born in Penzance, was not a writer herself, but as wife of the Revd Patrick Brontë became mother of a noted literary dynasty, the authors Charlotte, Emily, Anne and Branwell Brontë.

Cyrus Redding (1785–1870), born probably in Truro, journalist, newspaper and magazine editor, and author of novels as well as biography, and books on local history, travel and wines.

John Harris (1820–84), born near Camborne, poet who began writing while working down the mines.

Thomas Hardy (1840–1928), who trained as an architect before he decided to write for his living, was commissioned in 1870 to restore the dilapidated parish church of St Julio, Boscastle. While there he met Emma Gifford, whom he married in 1874. Although they later became estranged, after she died in 1912 he revisited Cornwall to revisit places they had seen on their courtship, and several of his poems written around that time are concerned with her death and memory.

Silas Hocking (1850–1935), born at St Stephen-in-Brannel, a minister in the United Methodist Free Church, later novelist with about fifty books to his name. *Her Benny*, a story about street children in Liverpool, sold over a million copies, reputedly making him the first English writer to achieve this feat in his lifetime. He is, however, little remembered today.

Joseph Conrad (1857–1924), novelist who sailed from the Tyne in 1882 on board the boat *Palestine*, which sprang a leak and was stuck in Falmouth for several months, an episode which inspired him to write the story *Youth*.

Kenneth Grahame (1859–1932) was staying at the Greenbank Hotel, Falmouth, in 1907 when he began writing the letters to his son containing the stories which were developed into *The Wind in the Willows* (1908). Toad Hall was said to have been inspired by Fowey Hall, and the rest of the story by Lerryn and the River Fowey.

Arthur Quiller-Couch (1863–1944), born in Bodmin, poet, novelist, editor of anthologies including *The Oxford Book of English Verse 1250–1900,* and *The Oxford Book of English Prose*. He was also a Professor of Literature at Cambridge University, where he was joint editor of *The New Shakespeare*.

Laurence Binyon (1869–1943), poet, wrote 'For the Fallen', including the lines 'They shall grow not old, as we that are left grow old, Age shall not weary them, nor the years condemn', soon after the outbreak of the First World War, while sitting on the cliff headland between Pentire Head and The Rumps, during a family holiday at Polzeath. Published in *The Times* in September 1914, it is often read aloud at Remembrance Sunday services. A large stone plaque was erected at the point in 2000.

Gilbert Hunter Doble (1880–1945), born in Penzance, church historian responsible for books on lives of the Cornish saints and local parishes, as well as an Anglican priest.

Virginia Woolf (1882–1941) regularly spent childhood family holidays at Talland House, near St Ives, which inspired the settings for three of her novels, *Jacob's Room* (1922), *To the Lighthouse* (1927) and *The Waves* (1931).

Crosbie Garstin (1887–1930), who lived at Lamorna for some years, wrote the Penhales family trilogy of novels, *The Owls' House*, *High Noon* and *The West Wind* which were set in the Penzance and Newlyn area.

'Sapper' (Herman Cyril McNeile) (1888–1937), born in Bodmin, creator of Bulldog Drummond and author of several spy thrillers.

Howard Spring (1889–1965), novelist who settled in Mylor and then Falmouth after he decided to become a full-time writer, was best remembered for *Shabby Tiger* (1934) and *Fame is the Spur* (1940).

A.L. (Alfred Leslie) Rowse (1903–97), born at Tregonissey, prolific historian, especially on Elizabethan and Shakespearean subjects, biographer, poet and occasional writer of short stories, and published over 70 books between 1927 and his death. He also twice stood unsuccessfully as a Labour candidate for Penryn and Falmouth in the 1930s.

Geoffrey Grigson (1905–85), born at Pelynt, poet, broadcaster, editor of anthologies, and writer of books on various subjects including art and the countryside.

John Betjeman (1906–84), Poet Laureate from 1972 until his death, writer on architectural subjects and broadcaster. He spent his childhood holidays at Trebetherick, often returned there as an adult, eventually bought a house there, where he died, and was buried nearby at St Enodoc's Church.

Daphne Du Maurier (1907–89), who lived in Cornwall from 1926 until her death and set most of her books in the county, among them *Rebecca*, *Frenchman's Creek* and *Jamaica Inn*, many of which were filmed for the large and small screen in the area. One of the county's most renowned writers, she also produced non-fiction titles such as *Gerald: A Portrait*, a biography of her actor-manager father, and appropriately, *Vanishing Cornwall*.

Winston Graham (1908–2003), who moved to Perranporth with his family during childhood, author of historical novels and thrillers, best known for the series of twelve Poldark tales, each subtitled 'A novel of Cornwall'.

William Golding (1911–93), born at St Columb Minor, novelist remembered best for *Lord of the Flies* (1954) and the trilogy *To the Ends of the* Earth (1980–9), the first volume of which won the Booker Prize. In 1983 he won the Nobel Prize for Literature. He spent his last years and died at Perranarworthal, near Truro.

Derek Tangye (1912–96), who lived near St Buryan for many years until his death and wrote the autobiographical *Minack Chronicles*, about his life with his wife Jeannie and the animals and birds with which they spent much of their time.

Jack Clemo (1916–94), born near Goonamarris, novelist and poet whose best work was inspired by the local landscape, although he went blind in his last years.

Charles Causley (1917–2003), born in Launceston, poet and compiler of anthologies, and was under consideration for the Poet Laureateship after the death of John Betjeman.

Joan Rendell (1921–2010), who lived at Yeolmbridge, near Launceston, local historian who wrote extensively on Cornish subjects.

Rosamunde Pilcher (1924–), born at Lelant, one of the most successful contemporary female authors in Britain for much of her career, with several of her stories set in the fictional town in Porthkerris, based on St Ives.

John Le Carré (1931–), born David Cornwell, lived at St Buryan for many years, renowned for spy thrillers including *The Spy Who Came in From the Cold* and *The Honourable Schoolboy.*

Colin Wilson (1931–2013), long-time resident of Gorran Haven, and author of *The Outsider* plus various works on true crime, mysticism, philosophy and other subjects.

D.M. Thomas (1935–), born at Carnkie, poet, novelist and biographer, whose novel *The White Hotel* (1981) was shortlisted for the Booker Prize.

Jessica Mann (1937–), writer of crime novels and co-author of *Godrevy Light* (2009), a non-fiction title, lives near Truro.

Martin Fido (1939–), born at Penzance, true crime writer, author of *The Crimes, Detection and Death of Jack the Ripper*, and biographer of Charles Dickens, William Shakespeare and others.

Tim Heald (1944–2016), biographer of the Duke of Edinburgh, Barbara Cartland and others, and author of the Simon Bognor crime novels, lived at Fowey for some years.

Nick Darke (1948–2005), born at St Eval, playwright, many of whose works such as *The King of Prussia* (1985), *Ting Tang Mine* (1987) and *The Riot* (1999), were based on local issues.

Robert Goddard (1954–), author of historical thrillers-cum-crime stories, including *Blood Count* (2011) and *Fault Line* (2012), lives at Truro.

Miles Tredinnick (1955–), who lived at Falmouth for some years, comedy writer for stage (*Laugh? I Nearly Went to Miami, It's Now or Never, Up Pompeii!*) and TV (*Birds of a Feather* and *Wyatt's Watchdogs*) as well as the monologue *Topless* and the novel *Fripp*. Under the alias Riff Regan, he is vocalist with the rock band London.

CORNISH EXPRESSIONS, SAYINGS, WORDS AND PHRASES

So near as the grave – Tight with money
So daft as a carrot half-scraped – Not very clever
Teasy as an adder – Moody
Two skats behind – Following up at the rear
Go like the mail – Go quickly, as in the mail in previous days
Dreckly – Later
Feet like half-crown shovels – Big feet
Myttin da – Good morning
Dydh da – Good day

Dohadjydh da – Good afternoon
Gorthugher da – Good evening
Nos dha – Goodnight
Mar pleg – Please
Meur das – Thank you
Dha weles – See you
Penn-bloedh Lowen – Happy birthday
Nadelik Lowen ha Blydhen Nowydh da – Merry Christmas and happy
   New Year
A wodhes kewsel Kernewek? – Do you speak Cornish?
Chons Da – Good luck
Da you genef dha weles – I am pleased to see you
Pinta hweg yw hemma – Lovely pint, this

CORNISH PROVERBS

A dry east wind raises the spring
Small riches have the most rest
A fog and a small moon bring an easterly wind soon

CORNISH LINGUISTS

Thomas Tonkin (1678–1742), Celtic language scholar who prepared a three-volume history of the county and a major collection of Cornish writings, which were however never published. His work in recording literary fragments of the Cornish language for posterity has been appreciated by several subsequent generations of scholars. He was also MP for Helston 1714–15, though he took little part in parliamentary activity as he preferred to pursue his academic interests instead.

Dolly Pentreath (*c.* 1680–1777), popularly regarded as the last true speaker of the Cornish language. Brought up as a Cornish speaker, she only learnt English rather reluctantly as an adult. Her last words were reputedly *'Me ne vidn cewsel Sawznek!'* ('I don't want to speak English!') However, in the mid-nineteenth century it was reported that a group of children in the parish of Zennor were being brought up bilingually and spoke Cornish among themselves.

Henry Jenner (1848–1934), Celtic language scholar, whose *Handbook of the Cornish Language* (1904) is often seen as the beginning of the modern revival of the Cornish language. He helped to found the Old Cornwall Society in 1920 and became its first president.

In medieval times, linguistic differences were fully recognised at national level and beyond. For example, Polydore Vergil, an Italian historian and churchman engaged by Henry

DOROTHY PENTREATH of MOUSEHOLE in CORNWALL, *the last Person who could converse in the Cornish Language.*

VII and subsequently Henry VIII early in the sixteenth century to write a history of England, wrote that 'the country of Britain is divided into four parts, whereof the one is inhabited by Englishmen, the other of Scots, the third of Welshmen, the fourth of Cornish people . . . and which all differ among themselves either in tongue, either in manners, or else in laws and ordinances.'

In 1531 Ludovico Falier, an Italian diplomat at the court of Henry VIII, maintained that 'the language of the English, Welsh and Cornish men is so different that they do not understand each other' and that it was possible to distinguish the members of each group by particular 'national characteristics'. Seven years later Gaspard de Coligny Châtillon, the French ambassador in London, noted that 'the kingdom of England is by no means a united whole, for it also contains Wales and Cornwall, natural enemies of the rest of England, and speaking a (different) language.'

EDUCATION –
THE BIRTH OF THE POLYTECHNIC

Derived from the Greek words 'poly' (many) and 'tekhnikos' (arts), the first use of the word in Britain can be traced to the Cornwall Polytechnic Society, founded by the Fox family of Falmouth in 1832. The first polytechnic was opened at 24 Church Street, Falmouth, later that year, and granted royal patronage by William IV in 1835 when it was allowed to add the prefix 'Royal' to its name.

Further Education Colleges

Penwith College, Penzance, founded 1980 from a merger of the sixth-form departments of Humphry Davy Grammar School for Boys, and Penzance Girls Grammar School. It was known as Penwith Sixth Form College until 1990.

Cornwall College, with the main campus at St Austell, and others at Camborne, Newquay, Saltash, Duchy College (Rosewarne and Stoke Climsland) and Falmouth Marine School.

Truro College, which merged with Penwith College in 2008 to become Truro and Penwith College, although both retain their original names.

Higher Education Colleges

University College, Falmouth

Truro and Penwith College

Camborne School of Mines, founded in 1888, merged with University of Exeter in 1993.

In addition to the above, in 2012 Cornwall had 31 state and eight independent secondary schools.

4

SCIENCE & INVENTION

SCIENTISTS, INVENTORS, GEOLOGISTS AND NATURALISTS

William Borlase (1696–1772), antiquary and naturalist, collector of antiquities, fossils and minerals, author of some of the first major books ever written on the subject in Cornwall, and rector of Ludgvan from 1722 until his death.

John Arnold (1736–99), watchmaker from Bodmin who became one of the foremost clockmakers of his day, made the world's smallest repeating watch and presented it to George III, who wore it set in a ring on his finger. Among his other inventions was a chronometer used by Captain Cook on his voyages.

William Gregor (1761–1817), metallurgist who isolated the calx (a residual substance that is left when a metal or mineral combusts due to heat) of an unknown metal which he named manaccanite. It was discovered almost simultaneously by another scientist, Martin Klaproth, who named it titanium; although Gregor had been the first, he accepted the latter name. He was also rector of Creed, and a skilled painter and musician.

John Hawkins (1761–1841), expert on mining and mineralogy, writer of several learned papers on local geology.

Richard Trevithick (1771–1833), mining engineer and inventor of the first high-pressure steam engine and first full-scale working railway steam locomotive.

Henry Trengrouse (1772–1854), inspired by seeing the shipwreck of the frigate *Anson* in Mount's Bay in 1807 to invent the 'Rocket' life-saving apparatus.

Sir Humphry Davy (1778–1829), chemist who discovered several alkali and alkaline earth metals, and invented the Davy lamp for use by miners in presence of inflammable gases.

William Bickford (1774–1834), inventor of safety fuse extensively used in mining.

Joseph Carne (1782–1858) mineralogist and geologist, manager of the Cornish Copper Company's smelting works at Hayle, where he collected specimens of copper ore, and published extensively in learned journals on mineralogy and metallurgy. His daughter Elizabeth (1817–73) likewise published geological papers in *Transactions of the Royal Geological Society of Cornwall*, articles in *Quarterly Review*, and several books.

Matthew Moyle (1788–1880), meteorologist and doctor who practised at Helston, became interested in mining through attending to men accidentally injured in tin and copper mines, contributed papers to various journals on associated subjects, and kept records for the Royal Cornwall Polytechnic Society at Falmouth.

Jonathan Couch (1789–1870), naturalist, author of four-volume *Fishes of the British Islands*.

Robert Were Fox (1789–1877), geophysicist who carried out research on the internal temperature of the earth, by conducting observations in the Cornish mines, and constructed a form of deflector dipping needle compass for polar navigation.

Sir Goldsworthy Gurney (1793–1875), inventor of oxy-hydrogen blowpipe and blastpipe for steam locomotives and engines.

Michael Loam (1797–1871), engineer who introduced the first man engine, a device to carry men up and down the shaft of a mine in Britain, and the forerunner of the modern elevator. Inspired by designs of a similar device already used in Germany, he won a prize awarded by the Royal Cornwall Polytechnic Society in 1841 and it was installed at Tresavean Mine, Gwennap, the following year.

Charles Peach (1800–86), naturalist and geologist, although not a Cornishman, undertook a detailed study of fossil organic remains on the county coasts.

Edward Budge (1800–65), author of papers on the geology of The Lizard, and rector of Manaccan from 1839 to 1846.

Richard Edmonds (1801–86), scholar of geology of the sandbanks between Penzance and Marazion, and on various other geological and antiquarian subjects, submitting papers to national and local learned journals.

William Lobb (1809–64), plant collector who introduced several garden shrubs and greenhouse plants to Britain and Europe from South and North America.

William Pengelly (1812–94), geologist and archaeologist, expert on local fossil fish, paleontology and human prehistory.

John Couch Adams (1819–92), mathematician and astronomer, partly responsible for discovery of the planet Neptune in 1846.

John Phillips (1822–87), geologist, metallurgist and mining engineer, involved with Royal Cornwall Polytechnic Society in pioneering experiments connected with electricity and the deposition of metallic copper.

Henry Bastian (1837–1915), physician and biologist, who published several major medical works including *Evolution and the Origin of Life*.

Frederick Betts (1906–73), ornithologist responsible for pioneering studies of bird life in East Africa and India.

Antony Hewish (1924–), astronomer and joint winner of the Nobel Prize for Physics in 1974, in recognition of his role in the discovery of pulsars, or rotating neutron stars.

EXPLORERS

James Erisey (late sixteenth century), born near Mullion, was a privateer and member of Sir Francis Drake's fleet, a cousin of Sir Richard Grenville, and took part in the colonisation of Roanoke Island, off the coast of North Carolina.

Richard (1804–34) and *John Lander* (1807–39), brothers both born and raised at the Fighting Cocks, Truro, joined expeditions in West Africa, and in 1830 they became the first Europeans to discover the source of the River Niger. Richard died after being attacked by African tribesmen when the wound became gangrenous, while John returned home to civilian life but died a few years later from the effects of disease contracted on his travels.

Samuel Wallis (1728–95), born near Camelford, circumnavigated the world in HMS *Dolphin* in 1766–8, sailing through the Strait of Magellan to Tahiti, then via Cape of Good Hope on the way back to England. His expedition discovered and charted several previously unknown islands on the journey north-west towards the North Pacific.

Edward Kendall (1800–45), polar officer, hydrographer, and naval officer, who took part in several Arctic expeditions, during one of which he discovered Wollaston Land, Canada.

5

CRIME & PUNISHMENT

CORNISH PRISONS AND EXECUTIONS

Bodmin Gaol was built, appropriately, by prisoners bringing large pieces of granite from Cuckoo Quarry on Bodmin Moor. It was opened in 1779 and closed in 1927 but has since reopened as a museum of penal life in the county, with a licensed bar and restaurant.

Between 1785 and 1909 fifty-five hangings were recorded at Bodmin. The last person to be executed for a crime other than murder was William Hocking, 55, convicted in July 1834 of bestiality, or as the contemporary press recorded, 'an abominable offence'. Prior to this date, most people who suffered the death penalty had been sentenced either for murder or offences such as forgery, robbery, arson and, in one instance, stealing a watch.

While researching prisons in the county on the internet for this book, I found a page headed 'Prisons in Cornwall', courtesy of Google, which began with the sentence: 'We have been unable to find any listings for Prisons in Cornwall. As an alternative maybe you would be interested in our listings for Public Services & Utilities.'

NOTABLE MURDERS AND
SUSPICIOUS DEATHS

William Wyatt

On 25 November 1811 Isaiah Falk Valentine, who made his living travelling around the country selling jewellery and purchasing guineas, was murdered at Fowey. William Wyatt, landlord of the Rose and Crown, had invited him to his premises a few days earlier, saying he had some items to dispose of. On arrival Wyatt took Valentine to the waterfront in Fowey, robbed him of £260 and threw him in the water to drown. He was found guilty in March 1812 and hanged in May.

John Barnicoat and John Thompson

William Hancock, a farmer, was accosted by three men while returning from Helston Market on 12 August 1820, and ignored orders to stop. Shots rang out as he fell from his horse, was beaten, robbed of cash and left for dead but picked up still conscious. The trio also attacked a labourer and his wife returning from market. They were wounded but recovered, and named Barnicoat, 24, John Thompson, 17, and the latter's brother Thomas, who were arrested. Before Hancock died he identified the two former as the guilty men. The trial of all three opened in March 1821, but as Thomas had not been named in Hancock's deathbed statement, the case against him was not proven and he was acquitted. Barnicoat and John Thompson were hanged at Launceston in April. Barnicoat may have been innocent, as he claimed, and another man of the same name, an itinerant farm labourer from Tregony, might have been the murderer. It is said that he fled to Australia to escape justice, but was so conscience-stricken that when he died there he bequeathed his estate to the family of his namesake in order to make amends.

Amy George

After Amy (or Emma) George, 19, of Redruth, had attended Methodist Revival meetings in the town for several weeks, her family found her behaviour increasingly odd. In March 1824 she had supper with her little brother Benny, 6, asked him if he would like to go to heaven, took a black silk handkerchief from a washing line across the room, used it to hang him from a crook behind the door, then went and told her neighbours what she had done. By the time they reached him he was dead, and she told them she was ready to die for her deed. At her trial the jury found her not guilty of murder, and the judge ordered her to be retained in custody, assuring her family and friends that she would 'not be kept long from them'.

William and James Lightfoot

Nevell Norway, 39, a merchant, was attacked and killed on his return home to Wadebridge after market day in February 1840. William and James Lightfoot, known for poaching and housebreaking, had been seen loitering in the area, and after being arrested and escorted to gaol, each tried to blame the other for the man's death. They were convicted and hanged in April. Norway left six children, all below the age of 9, and a widow Sarah, 36, who died apparently from heart disease, only six months after the murder.

Matthew Weeks

Matthew Weeks and Charlotte Dymond, both servants at Penhale Farm, near Davidstow, began walking out together until another youth, Thomas Prout, came to steal Charlotte's affections. In April 1844 she left for a secret rendezvous, presumably with Thomas, never returned, and her body was found on Rough Tor. At his trial Matthew confessed that on a walk together he accused her of disgraceful behaviour with another man, struck her with a pocket knife, and put the weapon away without harming her, but after further provocation he lashed out again and injured her fatally. His execution in August was witnessed by a crowd of nearly 20,000. A granite monument was later erected on Rough Tor, close to the scene of the murder.

James Holman

On Boxing Day 1853 the body of Philippa Holman, seven months pregnant, was found dead in her cottage at Crowan. When the well was searched and drained later that week, a bloodstained hatchet was found.

Her husband James, 29, a labourer, admitted he had murdered her, saying that when he accused her of drunkenness she attacked him, and he pushed her into the fireplace, but did not offer any explanation for the wounds he had evidently inflicted on her. He was hanged in April 1854.

John Doidge

Roger Drew, 57, a grocer and carpenter, was murdered at St Stephen-by-Launceston in June 1862. Suspicion fell on John Doidge, 28, an unemployed labourer, who frequented the same public house, the Smith's Arms. On the previous evening they were seen in conversation together. Doidge was seen early next day with a billhook which he tried to conceal behind a water barrel. He was found guilty and hanged in August, the last person in Cornwall to be executed in public.

Selina Wadge

Wadge, 28, was charged with murdering her two-year-old handicapped son Harry by throwing him down a well in a field near Launceston. At the time she was engaged to a labourer, James Westwood. When asked what had happened to Harry, she said firstly that he had died from a throat disease, then that Mr Westwood had taken the boy from her, killed him and also threatened her elder boy, five-year-old Johnny. Later she admitted killing the little boy herself, as Westwood had agreed to marry her on condition that she got rid of him. At her trial in July 1878 he denied it, she was convicted of murder, and hanged in August.

William Bartlett

William Bartlett, 46, a foreman at Calcarrow granite works near St Blazey, had an affair with Elizabeth Wherry, the nurse who had been attending his pregnant wife, and she bore him a child, a daughter named Emma Owen, in June 1882. Sixteen days later he strangled the baby, placed the body in a box and threw it down a deserted mineshaft at Lanlivery. In July he was dragged out of a large shallow pool beside a quarry, shouting, 'Let me die!' After he was rescued, the police made connections with this and rumours that a baby had been born in the area and disappeared, and the box containing the decomposed body was found. Bartlett pleaded not guilty at his trial, but the jury could not agree on their verdict. At a second trial, despite the lack of new evidence he was found guilty and hanged in November.

Valeri Giovanni

Valeri Giovanni, 31, an Italian sailor, came on board a Liverpool-based ship *Loxton* at New South Wales, sailing for Falmouth in December 1900. The only Italian on board, and unable to speak a word of English, he was teased by Victor Balieff, the cook. Giovanni stabbed him to death, was arrested, and at his trial in June 1901 he pleaded guilty, although on the advice of his counsel he then withdrew it and entered one of not guilty. In his defence it was claimed that Balieff had made numerous threats against Giovanni, but in his summing up the judge said it had been such a vicious assault that it was difficult to suppose one man could inflict such injuries on another without intending to kill him. He was hanged in July.

Robert Bullen

In January 1904 the body of gamekeeper Henry Osmond was found on Lord Falmouth's estate at Tregothnan, killed by a single gunshot. Robert Bullen, a poacher suspected of the crime, was brought to court in an ambulance. Witnesses spoke of the movements of both men on the previous day, and of a confession Bullen made to a local surgeon called in to dress a gunshot wound from which he was suffering. He said that Osmond had shot first at him and that he fired in return, but did not know whether he had hit Osmond. The jury returned a verdict of wilful murder against Bullen, who was sentenced in June to ten years' penal servitude for manslaughter. Three days later he was found hanged in his cell.

William Hampton

In 1908 William Hampton, 22, became engaged to Emily Tredrea, 15, and moved in to her family home with her at St Erth. Increasingly irritated by his uncouth habits, at length she realised that she no longer cared for him, admitting to a friend that she feared and hated him, and thought that if they stayed together he might kill her. In May 1909 she told him it was all over, and when she repeated herself the following evening he throttled her to death. Leaving her body propped up in a chair, he ran away, but a few hours later gave himself up to the police. He was found guilty and in July became the last person ever hanged at Bodmin.

Edward Black

Edward Black, 35, an insurance agent who had defrauded several customers, disappeared from his home at Tregonissey, St Austell, shortly before his wife Annie, 50, died apparently of gastro-enteritis in November 1921. An inquest revealed traces of arsenic in her stomach. After a nationwide manhunt he was arrested in Liverpool, tried to cut his own throat, was brought back to Cornwall, sentenced to death for murder and hanged in March 1922.

Ann Osborne

In April 1923 the bodies of widowed Annie Trenberth Osborne, 48, and her daughter Ann, 15, were found in their house at Union Row, St Teath. The heavily pregnant girl had been taken ill at church on Easter Sunday and was escorted home but refused all offers of help, and insisted that no doctor should be called. When seen a few days later she was clearly no longer pregnant, but looked very ill. Two doctors sent to the house by worried villagers examined her and confirmed she had recently given birth, but found no trace of the baby. After they left, her mother was seen bolting the doors and boarding up the windows. A day or so later a neighbour broke in and found the bodies. The inquest concluded that Annie was so ashamed of her daughter that she had cut the girl's throat and then taken her own life, but the baby's body was never found.

William Maynard

The battered and bleeding body of Richard Roadley, 84, a retired farmer and recluse, was discovered in February 1928 in his cottage at Titson, near Poundstock, lying on the floor wrapped in a blanket. A doctor confirmed that the injury was not caused by a fall, but he had been struck with a blunt object, and he died later that evening. The house had been ransacked, and the contents of the drawers were thrown around the floor. William Maynard, 36, a rabbit trapper at Poundstock, was charged with murder, found guilty and executed at Exeter in July.

Joseph Cowley

In February 1931 Mary Ann Dunhill, 79, was found dead, having been bound and gagged, at Pentowan Hotel, Summerleaze Crescent, Bude, where she was employed as housekeeper. The proprietors, Mr and Mrs Crisp, discovered her when they returned in the evening after being out all day, then went to look for their chef and handyman Joseph Cowley, 29, who was in charge during their absence. He was found in Plymouth the next day. On being questioned, he confessed that he had robbed the Crisps' rooms, then started going through Mrs Dunhill's possessions. She caught him red-handed, and to stop her from informing on him he gagged her, tied her up and ran away. At his trial for murder in June, he claimed he did not think she would die before Mr and Mrs Crisp returned that evening and found her, as he assumed that they would untie her in time. He was sentenced to seven years' imprisonment for manslaughter.

Philip Davis

In 1936 Monica Rowe, 15, moved in with her uncle and aunt, Philip Davis, 30, a turner and fitter with an engineering firm, and his wife Wilhelmina, 33, at Tuckingmill, Camborne. Davis was losing patience with his wife, probably suffering from depression after they had lost two children in infancy. When his wife and niece disappeared in April 1937 he told family and friends that they had left him, taking most of his money, but neighbours and police suspected otherwise. He rented a garage from his landlord, and was seen moving barrowloads of soil and stones inside later that day. A friend helped the landlord to search the premises, they traced a hideous smell to the inspection pit, and found human remains. Davis confessed to killing them with a hammer, was found guilty of murder and hanged at Exeter in July.

Gordon Trenoweth

When Albert Bateman, a tobacconist, did not return home from his shop in Arwenack Street, Falmouth, after close of business on

Christmas Eve 1942, his wife went there to look for him. Finding the door locked, she fetched the police who discovered his body on the floor. Gordon Trenoweth, 33, a local man with a police record for larceny, was arrested, questioned and charged with murder in the evening of Christmas Day. Among items found on him was a banknote torn and repaired with a letterhead by Bateman at his shop. At his trial in February 1943 the jury found him guilty, but 'with a strong recommendation to mercy', as they considered the killing was not premeditated. An appeal was dismissed, and in April 1943 he became the last man hanged at Exeter.

William Croft

Flying Officer William Croft, 32, station commander at Housel Bay, married with two children, had an affair with Corporal Joan Lewis, 27, a WAAF from Porthcawl. Realising one of them would have to be reposted, they resolved on a suicide pact. In October 1943 he shot her dead, but did not have the courage to take his own life, was tried at Winchester Assizes in November, and sentenced to hang, reduced to life imprisonment, from which he was released a few years later. For years afterwards witnesses reported seeing a young woman in a WAAF uniform, waiting for her lover to join her in death, sitting on a bench in the hotel gardens.

Bertha Scorse

Bertha Mary Scorse, 20, of Newlyn, met Joyce Mary Dunstan, 26, of Pool, at a tuberculosis sanatorium, and they became lovers. After they were discharged Dunstan returned briefly to her husband, then went to live with Scorse at the latter's mother's home. In January 1952 after Dunstan walked out, Scorse went after her and stabbed her to death with a dagger. She was tried in February and after two suicide attempts she was carried into court on a stretcher. Although found guilty, she was reprieved and is thought to have died in prison in 1995, after a history of being released and confined again for drunken behaviour.

Miles Giffard

Miles Giffard, 26, murdered his parents at their home at Porthpean, St Austell Bay, in November 1952. His father Charles, senior partner in a firm of solicitors, wanted him to follow in his footsteps, while he intended to become a professional cricketer, and was unwilling or too lazy to hold down a job for long. One evening Miles battered Charles unconscious on his return home from work. When his mother Elizabeth came home he attacked her, threw their bodies in a wheelbarrow, took them one by one to nearby cliffs and tipped them over the side, where they were discovered dead next morning. He drove back to London overnight to rejoin his girlfriend Gabrielle, but was arrested the following evening and confessed. During his trial in February 1953, several witnesses testified to his having received psychiatric help as a child. Nevertheless he was found guilty and hanged on 24 February.

Russell Pascoe and John Whitty

The bloodstained body of Garfield Rowe, 64, a recluse who lived at Nanjarrow, an isolated farmhouse near Constantine area, was seen in the yard by a neighbour on the morning of 15 August 1963 and reported to the police. Suspicion fell on Russell Pascoe, 24, an odd-job man and John Whitty, 22, an employee at Truro gas works, who lived at Kenwyn Hill caravan site, near Truro. It was proved that they had robbed the premises and fled with just £4 in cash, after killing Rowe to prevent him from testifying against them. They were found guilty, Pascoe was hanged at Bristol and Whitty at Winchester. It was the penultimate murder case on the British mainland which resulted in the guilty man (or men) being executed.

UNSOLVED KILLINGS

Jesse Lean, a miner and farmer at Trevarth, came home in February 1839 to find his wife Loveday severely wounded but still conscious. She told him that a man in a brown coat had forced his way into her bedroom and attacked her, and she died a few hours later. Jesse was initially the main suspect, but there was insufficient evidence to charge him, and at the inquest some said they had seen a man outside his cottage that morning. After a reward was offered by the parish for the conviction of the murderer, a neighbour made a full confession and was arrested, but he retracted it and was released without charge.

The body of Grace Andrew, stabbed to death, was discovered in her kitchen at Calenick in January 1830. At an inquest next day, it was concluded that she must have carried the earnings of her husband, who was employed in the local smelting house, around with her all the time, and that somebody had killed her to steal the money. In March three people living under the same roof were taken into custody on suspicion of murder, but released after questioning. Shortly afterwards Peter Matthews, a mason from Calenick, was arrested and charged. In court he maintained that much of the evidence against him was given by members of the Skewes family with whom he had lodged, and who had a grievance against him as a result of certain financial issues, and he was acquitted.

The bodies of Laura Sara and Joseph Hoare were discovered in January 1920 with severe head injuries, by a neighbour outside their smallholding at Skinner's Bottom, near Redruth. A doctor was called, but within a couple of hours both were dead. Hoare was a farmer and cattle dealer, while Laura Sara was his housekeeper and lover, separated from her husband for several years. Both were considered to be of loose morals and with a fondness for drink, and she had been convicted of keeping a disorderly house in Truro. The murder weapon was assumed to have been a log from the bloodstained pile near the cottage, but nobody was ever charged. At the inquest it was suggested that they may have had a violent argument, each inflicting severe wounds on the other, but the finding of only one bloodstained weapon made this unlikely. It seemed more probable that some unknown person had attacked Hoare, Laura Sara had gone to see what the noise was, and was killed so she could not inform on the assailant.

Alice Thomas, who lived with her husband William at Trenhorne Farm near Launceston, died in hospital in November 1930, a few days after being admitted with food poisoning. Annie Hearn, a friend of hers and her husband William, had recently lost her sister Lydia ('Minnie') to gastric complaints. When William returned home from his wife's bedside, he all but accused Annie of having murdered Alice, as she had been taken ill after a picnic at which Alice had eaten Annie's sandwiches. A post-mortem revealed arsenic in Alice's body, and an inquest returned a verdict of poisoning by person or persons unknown. The bodies of Annie's sister Minnie and her aunt Mary, who had died in 1926, were both exhumed and found to contain arsenic. Annie had fled, and after her clothes were found on cliffs at Looe it was thought she had killed herself, but she had taken a job in Torquay as housekeeper to an architect under the name of Mrs Faithful. After arousing the suspicions of her employer who saw her picture in the newspaper alongside a story about her disappearance, she was brought back to Cornwall and charged with the murders of Lydia and Alice Thomas. At the trial in June 1931, the judge instructed the jury to acquit her of both crimes as there was insufficient evidence to convict. William Thomas was linked to his wife's death, but again there was no evidence with which to charge him. One juror was allegedly heard to say later that the jury thought Annie and William might have acted together in murdering Alice.

SMUGGLING

Although the authorities regarded it as a crime, to many Cornishmen and women around the turn of the nineteenth century smuggling was a perfectly legitimate enterprise. Some of the episodes mentioned here doubtless contain elements of fact and fiction, embellished over the years. Nevertheless they also suggest that the forces of law and order did not always prevail over 'people power', the locals often taking sides with the people they regarded as free traders – and, one assumes, probably being rewarded in kind for their support. However, excise men and coastguards alike gradually kept a watch on the guardians of free enterprise, their tactics and hiding places, and by the mid-nineteenth century such clandestine activity had been driven underground if not entirely eliminated.

The Carter family

John Carter (1770–*c*. 1810), born at Breage, and his younger brothers Harry and Charles, were among the most renowned of Cornish smugglers. What little is known about their lives comes from Harry's autobiography, and from folklore handed down through the generations.

During the wars against France in the early years of the nineteenth century, the government increased taxes, especially on imported and luxury goods such as wine, spirits and tobacco, but owners of small fast boats could evade these if they could give customs officials the slip. Cornwall was an ideal smuggling base as it was so remote, and in turn it attracted wreckers as well. John was nicknamed the King of Prussia, as his operations were based around their home, Porth Leah, under a sheltered headland on the coast of Mount's Bay, which they renamed Prussia as he was said to resemble his hero Frederick II (the Great), King of Prussia. The place had slipways for landing goods, as well as cellars and lofts where they could store their contraband, and there was a network of people to store, transport and sell goods in distant markets.

Although operating on the wrong side of the law, they were devout Methodists and well known for their honest dealings as smugglers. Once during John's absence, excise officers removed a recently acquired cargo of tea to the Penzance customs house. When he came back, he and his men broke into the customs house late at night and carried off all the goods he regarded as his, leaving the rest alone. The authorities knew who was responsible, 'because he has taken nothing away that was not his own'. The Carters forbade swearing on their vessels, and when he was in Roscoff Harry held Sunday services on the quayside for his smuggling crew.

Smuggling in the area declined when the Carters' house was sold by auction in 1803 and a copper mine was opened on the cliffs overlooking the cove. Soon the income from the more legal trade of mining vastly exceeded that from smuggling. John and Charles retired into obscurity, while Harry became a farmer and full-time preacher. A coastguard station was built at Prussia Cove in 1825, and with this the gradually declining activities of the smugglers in this area then ceased.

Tom Potter

A leading member of the crew of a Polperro smuggling boat, the *Lottery*, who were arrested by the customs authorities in 1798 when they saw it becalmed half a mile from Penlee Point, and put to sea in several rowing boats. The crew of the *Lottery* opened fire while still some distance away. One of the crew in the customs boat died of his wounds, and their attackers became outlaws in their home town. The case came to court in 1800 when one of the crew, Roger Toms, was persuaded to turn King's evidence against Tom Potter, the man who had probably fired the fatal shot. He was tried at the Old Bailey and executed later that year. Toms, a brother-in-law of Richard Quiller, a distant relation of the author Sir Arthur Quiller-Couch, spent the rest of his life at Newgate Prison as an assistant turnkey. His action had made him detested and despised in Polperro, even by his own children, and he feared that if he ever returned to Cornwall there would be a price on his head. Nevertheless the incident would prove a decisive turning point in the authorities' efforts to end smuggling in the district.

Fyn and Black Joan

A notorious brother and sister partnership who smuggled goods from the Channel Islands to Looe Island in the eighteenth and nineteenth centuries. Joan was reputedly the more violent, and the ghost of one of her murder victims is said to haunt the island to this day.

John Knill

A collector of customs at St Ives Bay and mayor in 1767 who was not above a little smuggling himself. During his mayoralty he personally paid for the fitting out of a privateer to be used in such operations. One of his boats, laden with china, ran aground at Carrack Gladden. The crew escaped, and removed the ship's papers as they implicated Knill and a local squire, both of whom were naturally keen to cover their tracks. Another customs man at the town, Roger Wearne, tried to take some of the china goods himself, but as he was making his way off the vessel, a man nearby spotted his bulging clothes, realised what he was doing, and ruined his little subterfuge with a large stick carefully aimed at his pockets to smash his ill-gotten gains.

Hans Breton

A Dutch smuggler who used to drink regularly at the Blue Bell Inn, St Ives. He was said to be in league with the devil, and paid duty on only one keg of brandy which never seemed to become empty, lasting him over twenty years.

Robert Long

A seventeenth-century smuggler at St Mawes, who was eventually apprehended and executed. His body was hung in chains on the road from the town to Ruan Lanihorne as a deterrent to others.

James 'Old Worm' Williams

A St Ives smuggler who used to land smuggled Irish whiskey near the town breakwater, hiding it in fishing boats and pigsties close to the shoreline. One night in 1851 a coastguard in the local inn noticed three carts collecting the haul, but when he went to try to stop them he was set upon by a gang who bound and gagged him. He eventually freed himself, but by that time all traces of the contraband and carts had long since gone, and his efforts to prosecute came to nothing as he had no evidence against them.

'Cruel Coppinger'

A native of the north-east, who came to live in Cornwall where he thought smuggling would be more lucrative, and allegedly forced local villagers

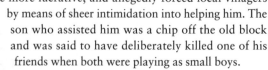

by means of sheer intimidation into helping him. The son who assisted him was a chip off the old block and was said to have deliberately killed one of his friends when both were playing as small boys.

Tristam Davey

A former smuggler turned innkeeper, he could consider himself fortunate to live in the days before his past would almost certainly have prevented the authorities from granting him a licence. He continued to indulge in what was obviously a lucrative sideline. One evening his men were rowing a cargo ashore, with a revenue boat in hot pursuit. He was familiar with that particular part of the coast, which the men steering the revenue boat did not know and were thus unaware of a reef of short slate rock running across the bay. Davey cleared it, but the revenue boat following him hit the reef and he shot the captain dead. As far as history relates, he got away with his crime.

SMUGGLERS' HAUNTS

Cawsand and Kingsand

Plymouth was always the most lucrative market for contraband in Cornwall, and goods were often brought into both coastal villages close to the county border so they could be ferried to the nearby town. In 1804 the revenue services estimated that about 17,000 kegs of spirits had been landed here in the previous twelve months.

Padstow

A beach about 2 miles west of the town was a popular landing point. In 1765 an informer wrote to the Earl of Dartmouth that one day his servants came across sixty horses from the beach about 3 miles from St Columb, each carrying three bags of tea weighing around 56lbs.

Pepper Cove

South of Padstow, a narrow entrance from the sea, fringed with jagged rocks, it was named after the boatloads of pepper landed there, which being subject to heavy taxation, was a popular commodity with smugglers.

Hayle

A popular disembarkation point for smugglers. North of the town are several landing points, including Hell's Mouth, and Ralph's Cupboard, named after a smuggler, 1 mile from Portreath, often used for storage.

St Ives

In or about 1870 *Old Duchy*, a local boat, smuggled large amounts of rum from Holland, until excisemen planted spies among the fishermen.

Lelant

Newcastle, a granite cottage at Trencrom Hill, was used as a beer shop in the nineteenth century, alongside which smugglers had excavated a cave for concealing their booty. The local church was used for a similar purpose.

Sennen

The local inn was owned by a farmer who ran local smuggling operations, with the help of the landlady Ann George and her husband, until the Georges quarrelled with him. In 1805 the excise men impounded a large cargo, consisting of about a thousand gallons each of brandy, rum and gin, and a quarter of a ton of tobacco. The farmer and his accomplices were almost certainly responsible and they appeared in court. The main witness for the prosecution was Ann George, but she was regarded as a malicious gossip and the case was dismissed.

Penzance

Another town where the mayor was also heavily involved in smuggling, and in 1770 the incumbent of that position was bound over with a large financial surety to desist from his activities.

Ludgvan

By 1748 smuggling had reached such epidemic proportions here that customs officers (presumably operating on the basis of if you can't beat 'em, join 'em) were unable to sell seized liquor, because the vast quantities already smuggled in were sufficient for the locals. Smugglers were asking 3*s* 3*d* a gallon for the illegally imported liquor, while the reserve price on the seized goods was 5*s* 6*d*.

Mousehole

Contraband was carried around openly in broad daylight. When asked why he had not apprehended those who were responsible, the preventive assigned to the town to try to stamp out the activity said he had been pelted with stones, and had to take to his bed to recover. Some of the Mousehole officials were charged with accepting bribes and cooperating with the smugglers, several of whom were described as being 'honest men' in their dealings although notorious smugglers.

Helston

Buildings were sometimes used to store smuggled goods in transit from the coast. One man, George Michell, took a cartload of silk up to the Angel Inn, but the landlady warned him that a party of searchers was waiting to seize him. He then sent his son round to the yard with the cart, walked into the bar, bought the crowd of searchers a drink, and engaged them in lengthy conversation. In due course they heard a rumble of cart wheels, and went over to the window, where they saw an old horse-drawn hearse driving off which they assumed must be going to a pauper's funeral. When the officers eventually came to search Michell's cart, all the smuggled goods had been removed.

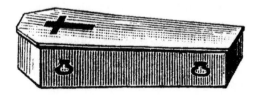

Mullion Cove

A popular landing place for contraband goods, associated above all with two characters. One was Billy of Praow, who was bringing a consignment of brandy ashore when officers from an excise ship who had been lying in wait came and captured it. News quickly spread, and a group of local people – possibly primed in advance to expect something of the kind – raided an armoury at Trenance, and used their stolen weapons to open fire on the ship until the officers admitted defeat, returned the cargo and fled.

Another, known as the Spotsman, was sailing home on one occasion from France with his cargo of brandy, and landed it at a point known as 'the Chair', between Predannack Head and Mullion Cove. When he was warned that the excisemen had been tipped off and were planning to mount a raid, he hid the casks in a mineshaft. Another time he was mistaken for a revenue man and shot by a fellow smuggler, but lost only his thumb in the encounter.

Gunwalloe

Caves on the beach were said to be connected by a tunnel to the belfry of the local church, while another passage linked Halzephron Inn to Fishing Cove, home of the notorious smuggler Henry Cuttance. There are other similar instances in the county, such as tunnels supposed to connect caves in the cliffs from Porthleven to Metherleigh Manor. At Penryn a tunnel linked the shore to St Gluvias' Vicarage, and further down the creek were two caves used for storage. Another tunnel nearby was discovered and blocked.

Falmouth

The town's docks proved popular with smugglers over the years. In 1762 three East Indiamen sailing from China to England anchored in the bay, and during the next two weeks ran a regular bazaar on board at which silk, muslin, china, tea, handkerchiefs and other general goods were readily available. Whether the operation continued until stocks were exhausted or the excise men put a stop to it is not recorded. Falmouth postal packet ships were also heavily involved in the smuggling trade. During the various wars of the eighteenth century, there were larger crews on the packet boats, which resulted in a sudden boom in trade throughout the town. As early as 1739, one trader remarked cheerfully on the prospect of imminent war that he hoped it would happen' with 'past experience teaching us that the Town will flourish in a French war.' (In fact the conflict, known to posterity as the War of Jenkins' Ear, would be with Spain, rather than France).

In May 1839 a schooner laden with coal undocked in the harbour, and after the consignment of coal had been unloaded a customs officer, suspecting something else, bored holes in the hull with a gimlet. He was immediately rewarded with a faceful of brandy, from a tub that had been stowed in a space between the false interior of the hull and the outside. When he and his men inspected further, they found 276 barrels of brandy and gin in the same cavity. His suspicions thus put an end to the clandestine trade of a ship which had been running this lucrative sideline for three years without detection.

Creeks to the south of Falmouth, particularly at Gweek and Helford, as well as beaches and small fishing ports at Porthallow, Porthoustock, Godrevy Cove, Coverack, Black Head and Kennack Sands, were also regular smugglers' haunts.

In September 1840 some excise men confiscated 126 half-ankers, an anker being a liquid measure of 10¼ gallons, of brandy from a ship landing at Gweek. As it sailed in, the crew called two men on the beach to help, not realising until it was too late that they were a couple of customs officers who arrested the smugglers at gunpoint. The cargo was held at Coverack, but a gang of thirty smugglers had the last laugh when they mounted a rescue operation a few nights later, broke into the storage premises after midnight, and removed all but three ankers which they presumably left out of goodwill for the officers of the law. A guard employed by the customs heard the doors being forced, but though he saw the heavily laden carts leaving, he was unable to stop them.

Fowey

In 1835 two coastguards went to Lantick Hill and hid in bushes near Pencannon Point in order to intercept a smuggling ship. At length about a hundred men arrived on the beach. One of the coastguards went for help, and when reinforcements arrived a party of six challenged the smugglers. One coastguard was knocked unconscious, but five smugglers were arrested. A party from the revenue cutter *Fox* came to help the coastguards, and captured 484 gallons of brandy, probably intended for the Crown and Anchor Inn on the quayside at Fowey, where the renowned smuggler Richard Kingcup had once been the landlord.

When the smugglers appeared in court, the defence argued that the clubs used in the fight were just walking-sticks. The local vicar was called as a character witness for one of the accused, and several farmers willingly vouched for the good name of the others. The jury acquitted them, adding a rider that they did not regard the clubs as offensive weapons.

Talland

The bay was a favourite landing point for smuggling boats from the continent. All that now remains of the village is the church high on the steep hill above Talland Bay. Near the door of the church in the south-west corner is a tombstone commemorating Robert Mark, but there is some doubt as to his identity. He may have been on a smuggling expedition when he died from wounds inflicted by a revenue man's pistol ball. A smuggler of the same name was sentenced in May 1799 for resisting arrest when the smuggling vessel *Lottery* was captured. Another account makes him a revenue man who was shot in a cellar on dry land, and Jonah Puckey, the ringleader of a smuggling gang, reputedly fired the shot that killed him. Of course, there may have been more than one man of the same name.

Whitsand Bay

The open beaches made a fine landing when the coast was sufficiently clear for covert runs, but smugglers seeking a more discreet approach headed for Looe, and brought the goods ashore on Looe Island. Ye Olde Jolly Sailor in West Looe was a smugglers' haunt, and the story has been told of how a landlady concealed an illicit keg beneath her petticoats and sat calmly knitting as her premises were searched.

PIRATES

In the sixteenth century, members of the Killigrew family were notorious for seizing ships, laying claim to the cargo and selling it in order to finance their lavish way of living. Piracy in England was then legal as long as it was done discreetly with as little bloodshed as possible and the minimum offence to foreign powers such as Spain, whose sovereign and authorities were always ready to protest to England about the exploits of her sea dogs.

There is some confusion about the Killigrews' feats, with certain achievements – or misdemeanours – being ascribed to different members. According to various sources Sir John Killigrew, the Vice-Admiral of Cornwall and reputed to be a former pirate himself, was entrusted with the task of keeping foreign would-be raiders away from the Cornish coasts. His wife Lady Mary was said to have led or at least directed several authorised pirate raids herself. In the 1580s (dates are disputed), she led a gang of pirates, or sent them, on to a Spanish ship, *Maria* of San Sebastian, which had taken refuge from stormy seas in Falmouth Harbour. They plundered the vessel of its cargo of jewels and silver, and massacred the entire crew. The Spaniards protested to Queen Elizabeth, who ordered the capture of Lady Mary, who was tried, found guilty and sentenced to death, but reprieved, probably because her admittedly sometimes over-zealous services to the crown as a pirate were indispensable. According to some accounts, she was only brought to justice after it emerged that her son, a judge, had tampered with the investigation into the incident.

A few years previously the appropriately named Lady Killigrew had also captured a German ship off Falmouth, sailed it to Ireland and tried to sell it plus its cargo there, but the ship owner was a friend of Queen Elizabeth and the zealous lady pirate was tried, sentenced to death and subsequently pardoned. Some sources say that Mary's first name was Elizabeth, so it is probable that different members of the same family were involved in similar escapades and facts have become blurred with the passage of time.

CANNIBALS

Cannibalism is fortunately rare among the British, and the last case recorded to date associated with the country was in 1884. In May that year a 19-ton, 52ft yacht *Mignonette* set sail from Falmouth. It had been purchased at Brightlingsea, Essex, by a Mr Want, who had planned to go to New South Wales but was no sailor himself and decided he would hire a crew instead, engaging a crew of four, namely 37-year-old Captain Thomas Dudley, Edwin Stephens, Edward Brooks and Richard Parker, who at 17 was the youngest. The vessel crossed the Equator in the middle of June, but foundered in a storm early in July about 1,600 miles from the Cape of Good Hope. The men escaped in a small dinghy, but within a few days they had run out of food and drinking water. After swallowing a large amount of sea water Parker became delirious, violent, and although he was already showing signs of emaciation, had to be forcibly restrained by the others from upsetting the dinghy. Towards the end of July Dudley decided that as Parker was the youngest, and did not have a wife or children, they would have to save themselves by cutting his throat so they could eat his flesh and drink his blood. Needs must, so Parker was accordingly consumed by the others.

A few days later they were spotted by the German barque *Montezuma*, bound for Hamburg, which took them on board, listened to their story, and placed them under arrest. As they could not be charged with any offence committed while on foreign soil (which the German ship counted as), they were taken to Falmouth, Dudley's home town, gave themselves up to the harbour police, were charged with murder and granted bail. People in Falmouth were so sympathetic towards the prisoners that a public subscription was opened to meet the costs of their legal defence, and raised £200 in less than three weeks. Brooks, the youngest, was judged the most innocent, and the Crown decided to use him as a witness against the others. They were tried in November, pleaded guilty and were sentenced to death the following month. At Holloway Gaol, they were told that the Home Secretary had successfully petitioned Her Majesty the Queen and commuted their sentences to six months' imprisonment, without hard labour.

TREASON

Robert Tresilian (1340–88), was born at Tresilian House, near Newquay. Sometimes called 'Cornwall's worst contribution to justice', as a young man he went to London, studied law, was appointed a judge and knighted in 1378. In 1380, shortly after the first poll tax was levied, he was appointed Lord Chief Justice of England. Within six months of the Peasants' Revolt he had condemned 1,500 peasants to hang for non-payment. Although he remained a favourite of King Richard II for a while, he fell from favour when he took part in a parliamentary commission to review and control the royal finances, something which the king regarded as an infringement on his prerogative. He was later involved in a case of espionage against the Duke of Gloucester, a dissident nobleman, and for several days he recorded the comings and goings of the duke's visitors, but was then recognised, arrested and summoned to appear at court at Westminster. In February 1388, when he was wanted for trial, he was found heavily disguised in hiding at Westminster Abbey where he tried to claim sanctuary. A mob dragged him into court, and as he had already been convicted of treason, he was taken to Tyburn where he was hanged upside down in chains.

CRUELTY

On 23 March 1864 *The Times* reported a case of maltreatment at the Bodmin Assizes. For eleven years Samuel Porter had kept his brother Robert confined in a single room. Without any fireplace or other means of keeping warm, the only furniture was a bed frame, and the only ventilation a sash window. Robert had had one change of scenery, when his brother moved house about a year earlier and he was taken to a new room at dead of night – in a wheelbarrow. When the Commissioners for Lunacy entered his room they found him behind the door squatting on his hands, his legs doubled up, his knees against his chest, his heels against his thighs, the feet crossed one over the other. There was no bedding in the room, and he had wrapped three pieces of sacking around himself to keep warm – the nearest to clothing he had. The stench was intolerable, and the floor was 'a miniature cesspool'. He was fed with ordinary family food served from a dirty frying pan, and tea from a filthy pewter pot.

In his youth he had been good-looking and intelligent, but when he was about 25 his mind gave way, and he had been insane for about thirty years. His father looked after him until he died in 1850, when a sister took over the responsibility. They treated him well until the sister went to America in 1853, leaving him to the tender mercies of his younger brother. A small weekly sum accruing from house property left by his father, about 7s, was paid to Samuel Porter for looking after him.

When the latter was tried on a charge of neglect the jury returned a verdict of guilty, 'but said they did not think the defendant was aware of the law, and therefore they recommended him to mercy'. In the view of the paper, 'no man could commit such disgusting brutality as Samuel Porter without knowing very well that he was violating some law, and that if the law of the land could not by some accident reach him it ought to do so'.

6

TOWN, COUNTRYSIDE & ENVIRONMENT

THE COUNTY AND COASTLINE

Cornwall is 1,376 square miles, or 356,265 hectares in area. It has more coastline, about 260 miles and with over 300 beaches, than any other English county. The North Coast Path goes from Land's End to Marsland Mouth near Bude, and the South Coast Path from Land's End to Cremyll, near Torpoint.

High Cliff, between Boscastle and St Gennys, is the highest sheer-drop cliff in Cornwall at 732ft.

Despite its extensive coastline, Penzance boasts the county's only officially designated promenade, which extends for just over a mile from the town harbour to Newlyn.

Bodmin Moor

Bodmin Moor is 80 square miles in size. It was originally known as Fowey Moor, after the river, until renamed by the Ordnance Survey in 1813. Brown Willy is the highest point on the moor, and indeed in the whole county, at 1,368 ft above sea level.

The beast of Bodmin Moor is said to roam the area, with occasional sightings and 'proof' in the form of slain and mutilated livestock. The Ministry of Agriculture, Fisheries and Food conducted an official investigation in 1995 but found 'no verifiable evidence of exotic felines' in the area.

The Roseland Peninsula

The Roseland Peninsula, sometimes known merely as Roseland, is a peninsula in the south of Cornwall separated from the rest of the county by the River Fal. 'Roseland' is said to mean 'the land of the promontory', Rhos being old Cornish for 'headland'. It includes the towns of St Mawes, and the villages of St Anthony in Roseland, St Just and Gerran. The sixteenth-century mapmaker John Norden wrote in 1584 that it was 'a circuit of land lying between the creek of Falmouth haven and the sea', and that it was 'called by the pretty name of Roseland, being derived from Rhos, the Celtic word for heath or gorse.' A more recent writer, H.V. Morton, observed in *In Search Of England* (1927) that 'If anything you have believed in has continued to be worth your faith, if anything you have wanted has not fallen below the expectation, you will realise my wonder when I saw St Anthony in Roseland (which) seemed lost, and happy to be lost, dreaming beside the sea.'

CORNISH PLACE NAMES

The Cornish name is in brackets, followed by its meaning. Where names have been altered over the years, today's name is given first.

Angarrack (An carrek)	The rock
Angrouse (An crows)	The cross
Baldhu (Bal dhu)	Black mine
Balnoon (Bal an un)	Mine on the down
Barncoose (Baren cos)	Wooden twigs
Bodmin (Bos venegh)	A monastery or monks' sanctuary
Boscarne (Bos carn)	Dwelling alongside a pile of rocks
Boscawen (Bos cawen)	Dwelling alongside an elder tree
Boscreege (Bos cruk)	Dwelling alongside a barrow
Bossiney (Boskyni)	House of Cini
Brea (Bre)	Hill
Burras (Ber res)	Short ford
Cadgwith (Caswyth)	Thicket
Callenick (Kelynek)	Holly grove
Camborne (Cam bryn)	Crooked hill
Caradon (Car Edon)	Fort of Edon
Carharrack (Car arth)	Fort on a higher place
Carloggas (Car logas)	Fort of mice
Carn Brea (Carn bre)	Rock pile
Carn Dhu (Carn dhu)	Black rock pile
Carnkie (Carn ky)	Dog-shaped rock pile
Carnmarth (Carnmargh)	Horse-shaped rock pile
Carnmeall (Carn Myghal)	Michael's rock mine
Carnyorth (Carn yorgh)	Roebuck-shaped rock pile
Carreck Loose (Carre los)	Grey rock
Carrick (Carrek)	Huge rock or boulder
Carthew (Car du)	Black fort
Carvean (Car byghan)	Small fort
Carvinack (Car meynek)	Stony fort
Carvossa (Car fosow)	Fort with walls
Carwin (Car gwyn)	White fort
Castle-an-Dinas (Castle an dynas)	Castle and fort
Chyandour (Chy an dowr)	House by the water
Chyangwens (Chy an gwyns)	House in the wind
Chycoose (Chy cos)	House by a wood
Chykembro (Chy Kembro)	House of the Welshman
Chynalls (Chy an als)	House of the cliff
Chynance (Chy nans)	House in a valley
Chypons (Chy pons)	Bridge house
Chyreen (Chy ryn)	House on a slope
Chysauster (Chy Sauster)	House of Silvester

Chytodden (Chy ton)	House by a grassland
Chywoone, Choone, Chun (Chy gun)	House on a down
Coverack (Goverek)	Place of small streams
Crowlas (Cores res)	Weir ford
Crows-an-wra (Crows an wragh)	Cross of the witch
Dawns Men (Dons men)	Dance of stones
Devoran (Dowren)	Watering place
Dor Catcher (Dor caja)	Daisy ground
Dorminack (Dor meynek)	Stony ground
Egloshayle (Eglos hayl)	Estuary church
Fowey (Fawek)	Beech grove
Gear (Car)	Small fort, or defensive enclosure
Godrevy (Godrevy)	Small farm
Golant (Golans)	Small valley
Goonbell (Gun pell)	Far downs
Goongumpas (Gun compes)	Level down
Goonhavern (Gun havrak)	Summer pasture downs
Goonhilly (Gun helghya)	Hunting downs
Gunwin (Gun wyn)	White down
Gwavas (Gwavas)	Winter pasture
Gweal Creeg (Cwel cruk)	Barrow field
Gweek (Gwyk)	Wood
Gwennap (Lan wenap)	Settlement of Wenap
Halwyn (Hal wyn)	White moor
Hayle (Hayl)	Estuary
Hendra (Hen dra)	Old farm
Henlys, Helston (Hen lys)	Old court
Kellivose (Kelly fos)	Grove beside a dyke
Kelynack (Kelynek)	Holly grove
Keverango (Kevranow)	Hundreds, or county divisions
Kerrow (plural of Ker)	Small forts
Kynance (Keynans)	Ravine
Laity (Legh ty)	Milk house or dairy
Landithy (Lan Dithy)	Settlement of Dithy
Lanhydrock (Lan Hydrek)	Settlement of Hydrek
Lanisley, Gulval (Lan Isley)	Settlement of Isley
Lanner (Lanergh)	Clearing
Lanuthnoe, St Erth	Settlement of Uthnoe
Lelant (Lananta)	Settlement of Anta
Lesnewth (Lys noweth)	New court
Leswidden (Lys wyn)	White court
Lis Escop (Lys Epscop)	Bishop's Court
Liskeard (Lys Kerwyd)	Court of Kerwyd
Lizard (Lys arth)	Court situated on a high place
Looe (Logh)	Inlet
Lostwithiel (Lost gwylfos)	Tail of the forest
Ludgvan (Luseven)	Place of ashes
Marazanvose (Marghas fos)	Market on a rampart

Marazion (Marghas byghan, or Marghas Yow)	Small market, or Thursday market
Melancoose (Mel an cos)	Mill in the wood
Mellingey (Melyn gy)	Mill house

Men an Tol (Men an tol)	Stone with the hole
Men Scryfa (Men scryfa)	Stone of writing
Meneage (Menegh)	Place of monks
Minack (Meynek)	Ground
Mousehole, formerly Porthennis (Porth enys)	Island cove
Nance (Nans)	Valley
Nancegollan (Nans golans)	Small valley
Ninnes (An enys)	The isolated place
Park an Grouse (Park an crows)	Cross field
Park darras (Park darras)	Door field, or a field by the farm door
Park Peeth (Park pyth)	Well field
Park Skibber (Park skyber)	Barn field
Park Venton (Park fenten)	Spring field
Pedn-men-du (Pen men du)	Headland of black stone
Pednvounder (Pen bownder)	End of a lane
Pencoose (Pen cos)	End of a wood
Pendennis (Pen dynas)	Headland fort
Pendoggett (Pen deu gwelenek)	Top of two copses
Pendrea (Pen tre)	Top of a farm
Pengelly (Pen Kelly)	End of a grove
Penhale (Pen hal)	End of a moor
Penhallow (Pen hallow)	End of the moors
Pennance (Pen nans)	Top of a valley
Penpoll (Pen pol)	Head of a creek
Penponds (Pen pons)	Bridge head
Penrose (Pen ros)	End of the heath
Penryn (Pen ryn)	End of the valley
Pentewan (Pen towan)	Top of a sandhill
Pentire (Pen tyr)	Headland
Pentreath (Pen treth)	Top of a beach
Penwith (Pen wyth)	The very end
Penzance (Pen sans)	Holy headland

Plain-an-gwarry (Plen an gwary)	Plain of the play, or playing place
Poldhu (Pol dhy)	Cove, or black pool
Polglase (Pol glas)	Green pool
Polgooth (Pol goth)	Goose pool
Polhigey (Pol heyjy)	Ducks' pool
Polperro (Pol Pyra)	Pyra's harbor
Polpuscas (Pol puskes)	Fish pool
Polruan (Pol Ruveum)	Ruveun's harbour
Polyphant (Pol lefans)	Frog pool
Polzeath (Pol segh)	Dry pool
Poniou (Ponsynow)	Bridges
Ponsanooth (Pons an goth)	Bridge of the goose
Pontshallow (Pons hallow)	Bridge on the moors
Porthcothan (Porth cothen or Porth goheudhan)	Old cove, or place of the happy, babbling stream
Porthcurno (Porth kerrow)	Cove of horns
Porthgwarra (Porth gwara)	Port of trade
Porthgwidden (Porth gwyn)	White cove
Porthleven (Porth leven)	Smooth harbor
Porthmeor (Porth mur)	Large cove
Porthpean (Porth byghan)	Little cove
Porthtowan (Porth towan)	Cove of the sand hill, or sand dunes
Portquin (Porth gwyn)	White cove
Portreath (Porth treth)	Beach cove
Portscatho (Porth scathow)	Harbour of boats
Praze-an-Beeble (Pras an pobel)	Meadow of the people
Redruth (Res ruth)	Red ford
Resoon (Res gun)	Ford on the down
Ridgeo (Resyow)	Fords
Rissick (Res segh)	Dry ford
Rose-an-grouse (Res an grows)	Heath of the cross
Rosemergy (Ros mergh gy)	Heath by a stable
Rosemorran (Ros moran)	Heath of brambles
Roskear (Res ker)	Ford by a fort
Roskruge (Ros cruk)	Heath with a barrow
Rosudgeon (Ros ojyon)	Heath of oxen
St Ewe (Lanewe)	Settlement of Ewe
St Ives, formerly Porthia (Porth Ia)	Ia's cove
St Just (Lanuste)	Settlement of Uste
Stennack (Sten)	Tin bearing ground
Tehidy (Teghyjy)	Place of retreat
Tolven (Tol men)	Hole in a stone
Tredinnick (Tre redenek)	Bracken farm
Trefrink, Trink (Tre Frynk)	Frenchman's farm
Tregarrick (Tre carrek)	Farm by a rock
Tregear (Tre ker)	Farm by a fort
Tregoose (Tre cos)	Farm by a wood

Trelowarren (Tre lewern)	Home of foxes
Tremellin, Trevellin (Tre melyn)	Farm by a mill
Tremenheere (Tre menhyr)	Farm by a longstone
Trenalls (Tre an als)	Farm on a cliff
Trenance (Tre nans)	Valley farm
Trendrine (Tre an dreyn)	Farm of the thorns
Treneere (Tre an yer)	Farm of the hens, or chicken farm
Trengrove (Tre an gof)	Farm of the smith
Trengwainton (Tre an Gwaynten)	Farm of the spring, as in season
Trenoweth (Tre noweth)	New farm
Trerice (Tre res)	Farm by a ford
Trevean (Tre byghan)	Small farm
Trevear (Tre mur)	Large farm
Treveglos, Treneglos (Tref eglos)	Churchtown
Trewarveneth (Tred war meneth)	Farm on a hill
Trewoone, Troon (Tre an un)	Farm on the down
Tywardreath (Ty war dreth)	House on a beach
Tywarnhayle (Ty war an hayl)	House on the estuary
Vellandreath (Mel an treth)	Mill on the beach
Vellandruchia (Melyn droghya)	Tucking mill
Vellanoweth (Mel noweth)	New mill
Wadebridge	Bridge by the ford
Wheal Owles (Whel als)	Cliff work
Wheal Rose (Whel ros)	Works, or mine, on the heath
Zelah (Seghen)	Dry place
Zennor, formerly Bosporthennis (Bos porth enys)	Dwelling at the entrance of an isolated place

CORNWALL'S TOP 20 BIRDS

The annual Big Garden Birdwatch, organised by the Royal Society for the Protection of Birds in association with the BBC over the weekend of 28/9 January 2012, used viewers' returns to compile a league table of the most frequently seen birds in people's gardens. The previous year's position is in brackets.

1 (2)   House Sparrow, 5.757 pairs per garden
2 (1)   Starling, 4.234
3 (3)   Chaffinch, 4.118
4 (5)   Blue Tit, 3.627
5 (4)   Blackbird, 2.190

6 (6)	Goldfinch, 2.104
7 (8)	Great Tit, 1.849
8 (7)	Robin, 1.490
9 (9)	Dunnock (Hedge sparrow), 1.405
10 (11)	Jackdaw, 1.322
11 (12)	Collared Dove, 1.153
12 (10)	Long-Tailed Tit 1.101
13 (15)	Greenfinch 0.998
14 (13)	Wood Pigeon, 0.968
15 (14)	Magpie, 0.956
16 (18)	Coal Tit, 0.944
17 (16)	Carrion Crow, 0.795
18 (-)	Feral Pigeon, 0.487
19 (19)	Wren, 0.482
20 (-)	Common Gull, 0.454

Absentees from the previous year's list are the Song Thrush (17 in 2011) and Blackcap (20).

The Chough

Although not common, the chough is in effect Cornwall's official symbolic bird, being one of the emblems shown on the county coat of arms. Legend has it that when King Arthur was killed, his soul entered that of a chough, and his blood stained its curved beak and legs red. A member of the crow family, it generally nests in caves on high cliffs. It was thought to have become virtually extinct in the county in about 1952, and a breeding programme was later established at Hayle. Thanks to careful cultivation of suitable habitat, it has bred successfully during the last few years, particularly in one or two locations which are heavily guarded to prevent the eggs from being stolen.

The Cornish Rex

The Cornish Rex is a breed of domestic cat, distinguished by its soft downy coat. It is a genetic mutation which developed from a litter of kittens born in July 1950 on a farm in Bodmin run by a rabbit breeder. One, a cream-coloured male named Kallibunker with an unusually fine and curly coat, was the first Cornish Rex. His owner then backcrossed him to his mother to produce two more other curly-coated kittens. The male, Poldhu, sired a female named Lamorna Cove which was taken to America and crossed with a Siamese, resulting in the breed having long tails and large ears.

The Scilly Shrew

The Scilly or Lesser White-Toothed Shrew is found in Africa, Asia, Europe, and on the Isles of Scilly, but nowhere on mainland Britain. Archaeological remains of specimens are thought to date back to the Bronze Age, although there is a theory that it may have established itself after some came on board ships from Europe or the Channel Islands.

BUTTERFLIES

According to the Cornwall branch of Butterfly Conservation, over 40 species are to be found in the county, of which 37 are resident, with three regular migrants and three recently introduced or re-introduced.

Resident

Brimstone

Brown Argus

Brown Hairstreak

Comma

Common Blue

Dark Green Fritillary

Dingy Skipper

Gatekeeper

Grayling
Green Hairstreak
Green-veined White
Grizzled Skipper
Heath Fritillary
High Brown Fritillary
Holly Blue
Large Skipper
Large Tortoiseshell
Large White
Marbled White
Marsh Fritillary
Meadow Brown
Orange Tip
Peacock
Pearl-bordered Fritillary
Purple Hairstreak
Red Admiral
Ringlet
Silver-studded Blue

Silver-washed Fritillary
Small Copper
Small Heath
Small Pearl-bordered Fritillary
Small Skipper
Small Tortoiseshell
Small White
Speckled Wood
Wall Brown
Wood White

Regular migrants

Clouded Yellow
Painted Lady

Introduced or reintroduced

Essex Skipper
Large Blue
White Admiral

Declared extinct

The Large Blue was declared extinct in 1975, its population having declined through the loss of habitat and food, mainly thyme flowers and ants, as a result of changes in modern farming. After extensive environmental restoration, it was reintroduced to the county in 2000 in selected areas. The Large Tortoiseshell was also believed to be extinct for some years but occasional sightings have recently been reported.

DAFFODILS

Cornwall's mild climate is a major factor in the county's position as the largest grower of daffodil bulbs in the world, with a total of 2,123 hectares allocated for the purpose, producing about 64,000 tons of bulbs per season.

THE DARLEY OAK

An ancient oak, believed to be over a thousand years old, stands in front of Darley Farmhouse, in the parish of Linkinhorne, near Liskeard. It was named after Thomas Darley, a landowner in the parish in 1727. From the eighteenth century onwards, parties were held literally inside the tree which at its base had a hollow cavity over 30ft in circumference, until fears were entertained for its safety and continued survival in the late twentieth century. According to legend, it has special healing properties if one meditates sitting against it, and that if anybody passes through the hollow and then circles its girth all their wishes will be granted.

ZOOS AND WILDLIFE PARKS

Bodmin Moor Wildlife Park
Monkey Sanctuary, Looe
National Seal Sanctuary, Gweek, Helston
Newquay Zoo
Paradise Park, Hayle

WILDLIFE AND NATURE RESERVES

The county is richly endowed with these, the following being the most important:

Armstrong Wood, near Launceston
Beales Meadow, near Launceston
Bissoe Valley, near Truro
Bodmin Beacon
Bosvenning Common, near Camborne
Breney Common
Bude Marshes
Cabila and Redrice Woods, near Bodmin
Chyverton
Gwithia Green
Gwithian Towans
Kemyel Crease, near Mousehole
Kilmanorth Woods
Kit Hill
Lelant Saltings
Loggan's Moor, Hayle
Looe (St George's) Island
Loveny and Colliford Reservoir
Luckett and Greenscombe Wood
Marsland Valley
Nansmellyn Marsh
Pendarves Wood
Penlee Battery, near Rame
Prideaux Wood
Priddacombe Downs, Bodmin Moor
Red River
Ropehaven Cliffs, St Austell
Seaton Valley
St Erth Pits
Steeple Woods
Swanpool, Falmouth
Sylvia's Meadow, Gunnislake
Tamar Estuary
Tywardreath Marsh

Upton Towans, St Ives Bay
Ventongimps Moor
Windmill Farm, The Lizard

THE EDEN PROJECT

Opened in March 2001, what rapidly became Cornwall's most famous visitor attraction is also the site of the world's largest greenhouse. Built in a former china clay pit 3 miles from St Austell, the Eden Project is run by an educational charity, the Eden Trust. It is dominated by three artificial biomes, each representing a different type of climate – the Humid Tropics biome, with rainforest and waterfall; the Warm Temperate biome, for Mediterranean plants; and the Outdoor biome, for plants which normally flourish in the Cornish climate. Between them they contain thousands of plant species collected from throughout the world.

THE LOST GARDENS OF HELIGAN

The Lost Gardens of Heligan, near Mevagissey, were created by members of the Cornish Tremayne family between the mid-eighteenth century and the early twentieth century. They fell into neglect after the First World War, but were fully restored in the 1990s and have since become a very popular visitor attraction. One of the driving forces behind their salvation was Tim Smit, later founder and Chief Executive of the Eden Project.

WEATHER AND METEOROLOGICAL RECORDS

Cornwall has the mildest and sunniest climate in England, because of its southerly latitude. A night-time minimum temperature of 23.1°C (73.5°F) was recorded in the county during an exceptionally hot dry summer on

4/5 August 2003, beating the previous record of 20.4°C (68.7°F) on 28/29 July 1976.

Winters are generally very mild and among the warmest in the country, with frost and snow uncommon in coastal and upland areas. The county averages 1,541 hours of sunshine per year, with 7.6 hours of sunshine per day in July the norm. It does, however, have a record for the highest wind gust speed ever recorded in England, with 103 knots (118mph) on 15 December 1979 at Gwennap Head.

The lowest temperature recorded in the county was -15°C (5°F) on 1 January 1979, at Bastreet, Bodmin Moor. On 13 January 1987, which was generally reckoned to be the coldest day of the twentieth century in the south-west, -9°C (15.8°F) was recorded at St Mawgan, and -6.4°C (20.4°F) on the Isles of Scilly.

Of all the occasions on which snow has wrought havoc across the county, none seems to compare with the blizzards of March 1891 when about 200 people were killed, mostly at sea, with 63 ships foundering, while on land more than 6,000 sheep and lambs perished. The outer harbour at Mevagissey was washed away, and telegraph lines between Penzance and Porthcurno suffered major damage.

Cardinham near Bodmin generally records the most rainfall in the county, averaging 54.6in per year over the last thirty years.

Drought

During the drought of 1976, after several months of unusually dry weather owing to a combination of very warm temperatures and high pressure throughout the country which followed an abnormally dry winter, no rain was recorded in most parts of Cornwall during April.

Floods and storms

Boscastle has long been prone to serious flooding, with floods recorded in 1847, 1957, 1958 (in which one man was drowned) and 1963. The best-documented is that which occurred on 16 August 2004 (coincidentally 52 years to the day after 34 people were drowned in a similar occurrence at Lynmouth, Devon) in Boscastle and the neighbouring village of Crackington Haven. Heavy thundery showers, remnants of Hurricane Alex which had crossed the Atlantic Ocean, were responsible for flash floods that afternoon. At the peak of the downpour, about 3.40 p.m., 24.1mm of rain, almost 1in, was recorded in 15 minutes at Lesnewth, while in Boscastle itself, 89mm (3.5in) was recorded in an hour. There was a corresponding rise in river levels in that hour to 2m (7ft). It was estimated that 20,000,000m³ flowed through Boscastle in one day, with the steep valley sides and saturated surface ensuring a considerable amount of surface run-off. No deaths or major injuries were reported, but about 100 homes and businesses were destroyed, while 75 cars, five caravans, six buildings and several boats were washed into the sea, trees were uprooted and debris was scattered over a wide area. A fleet of helicopters rescued about 150 people clinging for life to trees, roofs of buildings and cars. The phenomenon was very localised, with other rain gauges within a few miles showing less than 3mm of rain that day.

On 21 June 2007, Boscastle again suffered from flooding after a week of steady rain, with more intense localised rainfall and 30mm falling on the village and surrounding area within one hour. Roads were flooded, drains were blocked, and several properties were flooded by rain flowing down the streets.

On the night of 7 March 1962 gales and high tides battered Penzance, Newlyn and other nearby coastal resorts. About 300 houses were affected. According to reports received by the British Insurance Association, initial estimates of the damage to private property in Penzance and Newlyn amounted to £100,000, and adjusters were sent to the area later that same day to help householders with their claims. The Mayor of Penzance, Richard Matthews, opened a disaster fund, which in the first few hours reached more than 300 guineas, and the deputy town clerk said the town would certainly need government help to make good the necessary structural repairs.

Total eclipse of the sun

For those wishing to see or experience the total eclipse or full blacking-out of the sun by the moon on 11 August 1999, Cornwall was the best place in Britain, as the only part of the mainland apart from part of

South Devon which went completely dark for any length of time during the day. Temperatures suddenly dropped, birds temporarily ceased to sing and brief darkness fell at 11.11 a.m. For some, the effect was lessened by cloudy skies and rain, while others considered that watching live coverage on television provided a more picturesque experience of an event which would probably not happen again until 2090, but it failed to deter visitors who had come to the west country in their droves to witness this less than once in a lifetime experience. When many of them left Cornwall the following day, it was estimated that there were an extra 100,000 cars on the road departing from the county, the A30 being brought to a standstill at one stage with a 65-mile tailback from Launceston to Crowlas, near Penzance.

Environmental disaster

On 18 March 1967 the *Torrey Canyon* supertanker, with a capacity for carrying up to 120,000 tons of crude oil, ran aground on its way to Milford Haven as the result of a navigational error, and struck Pollard's Rock on Seven Stones reef between the Cornish mainland and the Scilly Isles. About 120 miles of Cornish coast were contaminated, and about 15,000 seabirds were killed, as well as a large number of marine organisms, before the 270-square mile slick was dispersed.

NATIONAL TRUST PROPERTIES

Buildings and gardens

Antony
Botallack Count House
Cotehele
East Pool Mine
Glendurgan Garden
Godolphin
Lanhydrock
Lawrence House

Old Post Office, Tintagel
St Michael's Mount
Trelissick Garden (see p. 92)
Trengwainton Garden
Trerice

Coast and countryside

Bodigga Cliff

Boscastle

Bosigran

Botallack Count House

Cape Cornwall

Carnewas and Bedruthan Steps

Chapel Porth and Wheal Coates

Crackington Haven

Crantock and Holywell Bay

Godrevy

Hawker's Hut (see p. 91)

Helford

Kynance Cove

Lizard Point

Mayon Cliff

Mullion Cove

Nare Head

Park Head

Penrose Estate: Gunwalloe and
   Loe Pool

Poldhu

Port Quin

Porthcurno

Rough Tor

Sandy Mouth

St Anthony Head

The Dodman

The Gribbin

The Rumps and Pentire Point

Zennor Head

LOST CORNWALL HOUSES

Carclew House

Built in about 1740 by William Lemon, a merchant who had bought the original estate including a smaller house. It was expanded further with the addition of new wings by his grandson William at the beginning of the nineteenth century. Largely destroyed by a fire in 1934, the remaining building was demolished and nothing remains apart from a few ruins and the terraced gardens.

Stowe House, Kilkhampton

Built in about 1675 by John Granville, 1st Earl of Bath, it was demolished some sixty years later after his grandson, the 3rd Earl, died in 1711 aged just 17 without an heir. The last member of the family to live there was a cousin, George Granville, Lord Lansdowne, who died in 1735. At a demolition sale in 1739 the entire house, except for the service quarters, was dismantled and sold by auction. All that remains is a faint outline of the main building, the Steward's House, now a farmhouse, the tennis court and some farm buildings built using materials left after the demolition sale.

Trebartha Hall

Built by the Spoures in about 1500, destroyed by fire and rebuilt in 1720. After use in the Second World War as a military hospital, the hall was near-derelict and the new owners demolished it to build a modern house.

Trehane House, near Probus

Built in the early eighteenth century for the Courtney family, it was destroyed by a fire in 1946, with only a few walls left standing.

Nanswhyden House, St Columb

Built by Robert Hoblyn, MP for Bristol 1742–54 and then a Stannator, it was reputed to be the most expensive house ever built in Cornwall at the time. He was a noted book collector and, in making his collection available for reference to all clergymen and 'gentlemen of taste', owned what was considered to be the first public library in the county. The house and its collections were destroyed by fire in 1803.

Tehidy House

Built by the Basset family probably around the twelfth and thirteenth centuries, it was sacked and destroyed during the Cornish rebellion of 1497 by a band of men angered by the loyalty of the crown to John Basset, Sheriff of Cornwall. Rebuilt by his descendants in the eighteenth century, and again in 1861, it was vacated after the family found it too expensive to maintain. The estate was sold in 1916 and the house became a tuberculosis hospital, was destroyed by fire in 1919 and later rebuilt, again as a hospital. It closed in 1988 and was converted into luxury apartments.

North Whiteford House, Stoke Climsland

Built in 1775 by John Call, High Sheriff of Cornwall, it stayed in the family until 1870, then passed to the Montagu family, and into the Duchy of Cornwall's ownership in 1879. Falling into disrepair at the turn of the century, it was demolished in 1913, with much of the granite being used for buildings now occupied by the Duchy College. The servants' quarters of the original house were used as accommodation for duchy staff until the buildings were condemned in 1968.

CURIOSITIES AND FOLLIES

Bodmin – The Dog Memorial

In 1938 Prince and Princess Chula (an Englishwoman, born Elizabeth Hunter) of Siam, now Thailand, came to Cornwall, lived at Rock for some time and then moved to Tredethy, a country house near Bodmin, which later became a hotel. They were joined there by his cousin Prince Bira. Both men served in the Home Guard during the war and Princess Chula became superintendent of the St John Ambulance Brigade. Prince Chula was a great animal lover, and had a granite memorial incorporating a drinking bowl for dogs, erected in the Priory car park. An inscription on it reads, 'Presented by His Royal Highness Prince Chula of Siam in memory of his friend Joan, a wire-haired terrier who died in 1948 in her 17th year. Further endowed in memory of the bulldog Hercules 1954.' Chula died in 1963 and his wife eight years later.

Bude – The Storm Tower

An octagonal building, built partly for ornament but also as a refuge for the coastguard, in about 1835, designed by George Wightwick who described it as being 'after the Temple of the Winds at Athens'. Sometimes known as the Pepperpot or the Winds Tower, it stands on a plinth with three granite steps up to the entrance on the east side, and the points of the compass carved as a frieze in sans-serif below the moulded cornice. It was demolished in 1881 as the condition of the cliff below had rendered it unsafe, and was re-erected further from the cliff edge.

Falmouth – Jacob's Ladder

A Wesleyan chapel was built in the town in 1791. It is said by some that Jacob Hamblyn, a builder, property owner and tallow chandler, thought that it was on too high a level for many would-be worshippers to reach easily, so he helpfully added 111 granite steps from the centre of town. He may have overlooked the fact that only worshippers possessed of exceptionally strong stamina would be able to scale them all at once and then attend a service in the chapel. The latter is now an inn, which some may feel offers more of a reward for those with the necessary stamina to reach the top. Others suggest that his real reason for building them was to provide access between his business at the bottom and his property at the top.

Falmouth – Church Street Shop Front

Built in about 1780, the shop at 54 Church Street has a bow-fronted window built in the early nineteenth century thought to be the oldest existing such front in Cornwall.

Falmouth – The Queen's Pipe

An incinerator built in the early nineteenth century to dispose of the large amount of smuggled tobacco being brought into port. As the trade diminished, the increasingly small amounts of confiscated weed were passed to the workhouse for the men there to enjoy.

Helston – Grylls Gate, Coinagehall Street

A Victorian Gothic gateway, at the entrance to Helston Bowling Green, erected in 1834 by public subscription to the memory of Humphrey Millet Grylls, a Helston banker and solicitor who helped to keep the local tin mine Wheal Vor open, saving over a thousand jobs in the process. A vellum copy of a eulogy written for Grylls by the Revd Derwent Coleridge was placed in a bottle and deposited in a hole made in the first stone laid as the monument was being erected.

Launceston – The Quarter Jacks

Sometimes known locally as the Black Jacks, they are two figures which wield their hammers on a bell by clockwork every fifteen minutes. Carved in the 1640s, they originally stood at Hexworthy House, a few miles south of the town. Later they were moved to a site over the old Guildhall, and after that to over the Butter Market clock, until the latter building was demolished in 1920 to make room for a war memorial. They were then placed over the Guildhall clock, where they can be seen to this day.

Morwenstow – Hawker's Hut

Parson Robert Hawker built a small shanty hut under the cliffs at Morwenstow, from driftwood which he had collected, hauling it up from the beach. Most of it probably consisted of wreckage from ships which had come to grief on the rocks. Naturally accessible only by foot, it is at present the smallest property owned by the National Trust.

Penzance – The Egyptian House

A house was built in Chapel Street by Plymouth architect John Foulston in about 1835, in keeping with a brief craze at the time for copying Egyptian motifs, and in imitation of the Egyptian Hall in Piccadilly, London. It was commissioned by John Lavin, a Penzance bookseller specialising in maps, guides and stationery, and dealer in minerals, who had bought two cottages for £396 and wanted to make something more picturesque out of them, raising the height of the two buildings now turned into one and adding the façade to the street front. In addition to carrying on his business from the premises, he also created a small museum of fossils and minerals inside. The building has since been turned into three flats, with two shops beneath, although the present owners, the Landmark Trust, have taken care to preserve the original decoration.

Saltash – Union Inn

In 1995 a union flag was painted on the front of the Union Inn, Tamar Street. Incorporating the red crosses of St George for England, the white and red diagonal crosses of St Andrew for Scotland, and that of

St Patrick on a blue ground, it was intended as a temporary measure to commemorate the fiftieth anniversary of VE Day, and was so popular with the locals that it has since been maintained. It also has two striking murals on the gable end, painted by local artist David Wheatley.

Truro – Trelissick Water Tower

A four-storey tower with fifty steps forming a narrow spiral staircase and only one room on each floor, it was built in about 1865 as a reservoir for Trelissick House. At the top of a tower was a bell rung at the start and finish of every working day for the benefit of the estate workers.

CORNISH WINDMILLS

Treffry Mill, Fowey
Mount Heman Mill, Landewednack
Empacombe Mill, Maker
Carlyon Hill, St Minver
Trevone Mill, Trevone

MUSEUMS, ART GALLERIES, HERITAGE CENTRES AND ARCHIVE COLLECTIONS

Bodmin

Bodmin Town Museum
Duke of Cornwall's light Infantry Museum

Boscastle

Boscastle Witchcraft Museum

Bude

Bude Castle Heritage Centre & Gallery

Callington

Callington Heritage Centre

Camborne

King Edward Mine Museum

Camelford

British Cycling Museum

Charlestown

Charlestown Shipwreck & Heritage Centre

Constantine

Constantine Heritage Centre

Davidstow

Davidstow Airfield & Cornwall at War Museum

East Looe

Looe Museum

Falmouth

Falmouth Art Gallery
National Maritime Museum

Fowey

Fowey Museum

Geevor

Geevor Tin Mine

Gerrans

Gerrans Heritage Centre

Grampound

Grampound & Creed Heritage Centre

Helston

Helston Folk Museum

Launceston

Lawrence House Museum

Liskeard

Paul Corin's Magnificent Music Machines

Lostwithiel

Lostwithiel Museum

Marazion

Marazion Museum

Mevagissey

Mevagissey Museum

Newquay

Newquay Old Cornwall Society

Padstow

Padstow Museum

Penryn

Penryn Museum

Penzance

Penlee House Gallery & Museum

Perranporth

Perranzabuloe Folk Museum

Polperro

Polperro Museum of Smuggling & Fishing

Porthcurno

Porthcurno Telegraph Museum

Redruth

Old Cornwall Society Museum

Saltash

Elliott's Grocery Store – based on a shop which closed in the 1970s
Mary Newman's Cottage – once the home of Sir Francis Drake's wife

St Agnes

St Agnes Museum

St Austell

St Austell Brewery Visitor Centre
Wheal Martyn Museum and Country Park

St Ives

St Ives Archives
St Ives Museum
Tate St Ives – the second regional gallery in the Tate Gallery network
Barbara Hepworth Museum & Sculpture Garden – managed by the Tate
   Gallery network

Torpoint

Torpoint Archives

Truro

Royal Cornwall Museum

Zennor

Wayside Folk Museum

CASTLES

Bossiney, a late eleventh-century fortress, built by Robert, Count of
Mortain, half-brother of William the Conqueror, long since ruined.

Bottreaux, built in the late twelfth century for the Bottreaux family, who
came from Normandy around the time of the conquest. A stone motte and
bailey fortress, it was a ruin by the late fifteenth century with only a few
earthworks remaining. Boscastle takes its name from an abbreviated form
of 'Bottreaux Castle'.

Caerhays, near Mevagissey, a semi-castellated manor house built
between 1807 and 1810 by John Nash on the site of a former dwelling,
incorporating parts of the older construction, with the ancient chapel still
preserved.

Cardinham, a large eleventh-century earth ringwork and bailey fortress, built probably by Richard Fitz Turold, Sheriff of Cornwall for the Earl of Cornwall, Robert de Mortain who was William the Conqueror's half-brother. It was in ruins by the fifteenth century, possibly earlier.

Carn Brea, a fourteenth-century stone twin-towered fortress originally built as a chapel, remodelled in the eighteenth century as a hunting lodge in the style of a castle. In about 1900 the then tenant agreed to display a light in the north facing window so it could be used as a beacon for ships. In the 1980s it was refurbished as a restaurant.

Castle Dore, a small circular fort dating from around 200 BC, probably abandoned soon after the Roman invasion of Britain but reoccupied in the fifth or sixth centuries. The site was used as a camp in 1644 by the Parliamentarian army, under the Earl of Essex.

Chun, an Iron Age hill fort near Land's End built two or three centuries BC, was probably occupied before and after the Roman occupation. Around 280ft in diameter, the fort is encircled by a double drystone rampart of granite with external ditches, and remains of huts built in the Dark Ages can still be seen.

Cliff Castle, Trevelgue Head, Newquay, is an Iron Age promontory fort, originally defended by six ramparts and ditches, occupied until the Middle Ages.

Helston, a thirteenth-century castle built by Edmund of Cornwall, probably as a fortified manor house, but ruined by the late fifteenth century.

Horneck, or Hornocke, believed to have been near Penzance, but no remains exist.

Ince, near Saltash, a seventeenth-century manor house, sometimes not regarded by military historians as a genuine castle, built at about the time of the outbreak of the Civil War

Launceston Castle, an eleventh-century motte and bailey wooden castle. Built by Robert, Count of Mortain on a mound overlooking the town, and initially known as Dunheved Castle, it was first used as administrative headquarters by the Earls of Cornwall for their estates. During the Civil War it was loyal to the Royalist cause until it fell to Cromwell's forces in 1645. It later became a prison and the site of the county assizes and gaol, where trials and executions were held until 1821. After the gaol was demolished, the castle ruins were landscaped and became a public park and garden, used briefly by American soldiers in the Second World War as a hospital.

Maen, an Iron Age promontory fort and the most westerly castle site in England, was probably built around 500 BC. Pottery fragments thought to date from 400 BC to AD 400 have been found on the site.

Pendennis, one of a chain of castles built by Henry VIII between 1539 and 1545 to counter an invasion threat from Catholic France and Spain, faces St Mawes Castle across Falmouth Harbour. During the Civil War it was one of the last British garrisons to surrender to Cromwell.

Pengersick, fortified Tudor manor house at Praa Sands between Helston and Penzance, reputedly the most haunted castle in Britain, boasts a newel stair regarded as one of the best examples anywhere in the country.

Restormel, a twelfth-century stone castle, built on an earlier Norman motte and bailey fort probably by Richard, Earl of Cornwall, when he moved his main administrative centre to Restormel from Launceston Castle. During the Civil War Royalist forces routed the Parliamentarian garrison.

St Catherine's, a two-storey coastal fort, built in about 1540 by Henry VIII, replacing two earlier blockhouses on opposite sides of the estuary Fowey and Polruan.

St Mawes, another of Henry VIII's defensive structures, and the most elaborately decorated of all, guarded the anchorage of Carrick Roads, and was designed to mount heavy ship-sinking guns. Its defences were improved during the reign of Elizabeth I after a Spanish raid on Penzance in 1595; in case of invasion. It came under attack during the Civil War, when the governor surrendered at once. Until the Second World War it was still used as a gun emplacement to protect Falmouth harbour.

St Michael's Mount, Mounts Bay, on top of a small island connected to the mainland by a causeway that appears only at low tide, has at various times been a priory, fortress, and place of pilgrimage. Edward

the Confessor granted the mount to Benedictine monks from Mont St Michel in France. In the twelfth century they built a priory on the summit, as well as constructing a harbour and causeway. In the reign of Richard I it was captured on behalf of his brother Prince John, later King John, and in 1473 John de Vere, Earl of Oxford, held it during a siege lasting almost six months against a 6,000-strong force of Edward IV. Humphry Arundell, the governor of St Michael's Mount, was one of the leaders of the Cornish Prayer Book rebellion of 1549. Seized during the dissolution of the monasteries, it became a fortress and was threatened during the Spanish raid on Mounts Bay. During the Civil War, Sir Arthur Basset held it against the Parliamentary forces until it was captured in 1646 by Colonel John St Aubyn, who bought it from the state in 1659. Now a National Trust property, it has remained the family home of his descendants ever since.

Tintagel, once the legendary home of King Arthur, was built in about 1233 by Richard, Earl of Cornwall, but ruined and abandoned probably in the late fifteenth century.

Trematon was begun in the eleventh century and completed about two hundred years later. The original building was the Black Prince's favourite Cornish castle and he was a regular visitor when travelling to and from France to fight in the Hundred Years' War. Sir Francis

Drake is believed to have used it to store his plunder captured from the Spanish during his raids in 1580, most of which was sent to London as a gift for Elizabeth I. Part of the original castle wall was demolished in the early nineteenth century to give a view of the countryside when the Georgian house was built. It remains a private home, a striking combination of medieval castle and Regency mansion.

ROMAN FORTS

Excluding those listed under castles above, there are traces of almost 80 ancient hill forts in Cornwall. All were built in the Iron Age, the Roman era or shortly afterwards. Most have shown some evidence of occupation by the Cornish, or Cornovii.

Allabury

St Agnes Beacon

St Allen

Ash Bury

Bake Rings, Pelynt

Berry Castle, St Neot

Bishop's Wood, Truro

Black Tor, Temple

Bury Down, Lanreath

Blacketon Rings

Bosigran Castle

Cadson Bury, Newbridge

Caer Bran

Caer Dane, Perranzabuloe

Caer Kief, settlement enclosure, Perranzabuloe

Caervallack, Mawgan-in-Meneage

Carlidnack, settlement enclosure, Mawnan Smith

Carne Beacon, round barrow, Veryan

Carvossa, settlement enclosure, Probus

Carwynnen Quoit, Penwith

Castle an Dinas

Castlewich, Callington

St Columb Major

Castle Killibury Camp

Castle Pencaire, Germoe

Chynhalls Point, Coverack

Craddock Moor, Minions

Crane Castle, Portreath

Crowpound, St Neot

St Cuby's Church

Dean Point

Demelza Castle

St Dennis Hill Fort

Dingerein Castle, Gerrans

Dodman Point

Dry Tree, Goonhilly

St Dominick Hillfort

Duloe

Dunmere Fort

Dunterton Hillfort

Faughan

Four Barrows, Silverwell

Gear Fort

Golden, Probus

Gurnard's Head

Hall Rings, Pelynt
Helbury Castle
Hilton Wood Castle
Kelly Rounds
Kelsey Head, Cubert
Kenidjack Castle
Kenwyn Hillfort
Kestle Rings
Ladock Hillfort
Largin Castle, West
    Taphouse
Lescudjack Hill Fort
Lesingey Round
Liveloe
Maen Castle
Nattlebury
St Newlyn East
St Newlyn East, Fiddlers
    Green

Padderbury
Pencarrow Rounds
Penhale Point, Cubert
Penhargard Castle
Polyphant Hillfort
Prideaux Castle
Prospidnick Hill
Rame Head
Redcliff Castle
Resugga Castle
Rough Tor
Round Wood, Feock
The Rumps
St Piran's Round,
    settlement enclosure
Stowe's Pound
St Stephens Beacon
Trebowland Round,
    settlement, Gwennap

Tregarrick Tor
Trereen Dinas
Tregeare Rounds
Trelaske Hillfort
Trencrom Hill
Treryn Dinas
Tresawsen,
    Perranzabuloe
Trevelque Head
Trewinnion
Trewardreva
Treyarnon Fort
Veryan Castle, settlement
    enclosure
Warbstow Bury
Yearle's Wood

OTHER PREHISTORIC SITES

Bolster Bank, earthwork, St Agnes
Giant's Hedge, earthwork from Lerryn past Lanreath to near West Looe
Goonzion, settlement enclosure near St Neot
The Hurlers, stone circles, near Minions
Rillaton, round barrow, near Minions
Taphouse Ridge, tound barrow cemetery, near West Taphouse

ISLANDS

The Carracks and *Little Carracks*, a group of small rocky inshore islands off the Atlantic north coast, between Zennor and St Ives.

Godrevy Island, off Godrevy Point, on the eastern side of St Ives Bay, about 3 miles north-east of Hayle.

Longships, a group of rocky islands 1½ miles west of Land's End. All but the three largest, Tal-y-Maen, Carn Bras and Meinek, are usually submerged at high water.

Looe Island, or St George's Island, or St Michael's Island, a mile from Looe, about 22.5 acres in area and 154ft above sea level at the highest point.

Mullion Island, about half a mile from Mullion, 118ft above high water level.

The Isles of Scilly, an archipelago of five inhabited islands and about 140 small rocky islets, about 28 miles west of Land's End. The inhabited islands, in order of area, with the 2001 census populations, are St Mary's (1,666); Tresco (180); St Martin's (142); Bryher (92) and St Agnes (73). A sixth, Samson, was inhabited until 1855, when the remaining two families were removed by the Lord Proprietor as they were suffering from severe deprivation and malnutrition, thought to be the result of their meagre diet of limpets and potatoes.

St Clement's Isle, a small rocky islet jutting from the coast outside Mousehole Harbour.

St Michael's Mount, known locally as simply The Mount, a tidal island off the coast near Marazion.

Seghy, a large rock in Cripp's Cove, about a mile west of Porthcurno.

Wolf Rock, about 4 miles south-west of Land's End.

CORNISH RIVERS

Allen

There are two Allen rivers in Cornwall. One rises north of St Allen and flows southwards through the Idless Valley into Truro, where it joins the River Kenwyn to form the River Truro. The other, a major tributary of the Camel, springs north-east of Camelford and flows south-west through the Allen Valley, passing St Teath and St Kew Highway, and into the River Camel near Sladesbridge.

Camel

Rises on the edge of Bodmin Moor and enters the Atlantic Ocean between Stepper Point and Pentire Point.

Cober

Rises near Porkellis Moor and flows into the River Helston, then enters Loe Pool.

De Lank

A tributary of the Camel, it rises from Rough Tor Marsh between the two highest peaks on Bodmin Moor, Rough Tor and Brown Willy, then flows south-west into the Camel.

Fal

Flows through Cornwall, rising on Goss Moor and into the English Channel at Falmouth, separating the Roseland peninsula from the rest of the county.

Fowey

Rises north-west of Brown Willy, close to a tributary rising at Dozmary Pool and Colliford Lake, flows past Lanhydrock House, Restormel Castle and Lostwithiel, then becomes wider at Milltown and flows into the English Channel at Fowey. It has seven tributaries, including the Lerryn, the largest, St Neot, and Warleggan.

Gannel

Rises in Indian Queens, flows north, becomes a tidal estuary dividing Newquay and Crantock, and then joins the Celtic Sea.

Gover Stream

Has its source on the north-east of Blackpool China Clay pit, then flows south-east through Gover Valley into St Austell where it joins the St Austell River, of which it is a tributary.

Hamoaze

An estuarine stretch of the River Tamar, between the Lynher and Plymouth Sound.

Hayle

Rises south-west of Crowan, flows through a steep wooded valley north of Trescowe Common, then north near Relubbus, past St Erth, and into St Ives Bay.

Helford

A ria, or flooded valley, rather than a true river, fed by small streams into its seven creeks, namely Ponsontuel, Mawgan, Polpenwith, Polwheveral, Frenchman's (immortalised by Daphne Du Maurier's novel *Frenchman's Creek*), Port Navas and Gillan.

Inny

A tributary of the River Tamar, has its source near Davidstow, east of Bodmin Moor, then meets the Tamar at Inny Foot near Dunterton.

Looe

Flows into the English Channel at Looe. It has two main branches, the East Looe and West Looe Rivers. The eastern tributary has its source near St Cleer and flows south, passing close to the western outskirts of Liskeard. The western tributary has its source near Dobwalls. The lowest stretch of the rivers form the Looe Estuary.

Lynher, or St Germans River

Flows through east Cornwall, passing St Germans and entering the River Tamar at the Hamoaze, which flows into Plymouth Sound. It has several main tributaries, the largest being the River Tiddy, also Deans Brook and Withey Brook.

Menalhyl

Flows north-west through St Columb Major and Mawgan-in-Pydar, and enters the sea at Mawgan Porth.

Mylor Creek

A tributary of the River Fal, 2 miles north of Falmouth, which forms an inland tidal lake.

Ottery

Has its source south-east of Otterham, and flows into the Tamar north-east of Launceston.

Par

A river formed by several streams, rising near the villages of Lockengate, Lanivet and Tregullon, which flow south into the English Channel at Par.

Pont Creek

Also known as Pont Pill, joins the River Fowey at Penleath Point.

Port Navas Creek

One of seven creeks off Helford River.

Red

The county has two Red Rivers. One rises from springs near Bolenowe, flows north through a gorge west of Carn Brea, and into St Ives Bay at

Godrevy on the Atlantic Coast. The second rises at Towednack, flows south-east through Ludgvan, then south-west into Mount's Bay at Marazion.

Restronguet Creek

A tidal ria and a tributary of Carrick Roads, the estuary of the Fal, between Truro and Falmouth. It forms the boundary between the parishes of Feock, Mylor and Perranarworthal.

St Austell

Also known as the River Vinnick, and sometimes the White River as waste water from china clay quarrying and refining practices often turned it white, it drains the central southern section of St Austell Moorland. It has two main tributaries, the first of which begins south of Hensbarrow Beacon, flows to Carthew, heads south, passes Ruddlemoor and Trethowel, passes under the Cornish main line railway and into St Austell. The second begins at Longstone Moor, flows south to a viaduct under the Cornish main line railway, then turns south-east, flows into St Austell and joins the Trenance Valley River. It then flows south along the Pentewan Valley and enters the English Channel at Pentewan.

Tamar

This river forms most of the border between Cornwall and Devon, and flows southwards into the Hamoaze, then enters Plymouth Sound. Its Cornish tributaries include the rivers Inny, Ottery, Kensey and Lynher, and in Devon the Deer and Tavy.

Tiddy

The main tributary of the River Lynher, it rises near Pensilva and flows south-east past Tideford (taking its name from 'Ford on the River Tiddy'), then joins the Lynher.

Truro

Named after the city through which it runs, this river is the product of the convergence of the Rivers Kenwyn and Allen, flows into the Fal and then into the Carrick Roads.

Valency

A river with several tributaries, including the River Jordan, it flows past Lesnewth and enters the sea at Boscastle.

7

TRANSPORT, BUSINESS, INDUSTRY & POPULATION

RAILWAYS

The first railway built in the county, between Hayle and Portreath, was opened on 29 December 1837. It was primarily a mineral transport route but also carried passengers. A main line to Redruth and branch lines to Pool, Portreath, Roskear, North Crofty and Tresavean were added. Full passenger services were introduced on the main line in 1843, and three years later the West Cornwall Railway was formed to operate the existing line between Hayle and Redruth, and extend the service to Truro and Penzance. In 1866 it was leased to the Great Western Railway, and nationalised in 1948 when it became part of the responsibility of British Railways.

The main Cornwall Railway had been planned in 1835 with proposals for a line from London to Falmouth, but building was delayed by lack of finance. Work on construction at various places was halted in 1848 but resumed four years later. The Royal Albert Bridge at Saltash, designed by Isambard Kingdom Brunel, was opened in 1859, followed later that week by the Plymouth to Truro line, with a line from Truro to Falmouth in 1863. It was amalgamated with the Great Western Railway in 1889, and nationalised in 1948.

CORNWALL RAILWAY MAIN LINE STATIONS, INCLUDING THOSE NOW CLOSED AND UNMANNED HALTS

Saltash (opened 1859)
Defiance Platform (1905–30), serving naval personnel on HMS
    Defiance
St Germans (1859)
Menheniot (1859)
Liskeard (1859)
Doublebois (1860–1964)
Bodmin Parkway, previously Bodmin Road (1859)
Lostwithiel (1859)
Par (1859)
St Austell (1859)
Burngullow (1863)
Grampound Road (1859)
Probus and Ladock Platform (1908–57)
Truro (1859) – jointly with West Cornwall Railway
Perranwell (1863) – formerly Perran
Penryn (1863)
Penmere Platform (1925)
Falmouth (1863)
Falmouth, The Dell (1970)

WEST CORNWALL AND HAYLE RAILWAY STATIONS

Newham (1855–63)
Truro (1859)
Truro Road (1852–5)
Chacewater (1852–1964)
Scorrier – also known as Scorrier Gate (1852–1964)
Redruth (1852)
Pool (1852–1961) – also known as Carn Brea
Dolcoath Halt (1905–8)
Camborne (1843)

Penponds (1843–52)
Gwinear Road (1843–64)
Angarrack (1843–52)
Copperhouse (1843–52)
Hayle (1852)
St Erth (1852) – formerly St Ives Road
Marazion (1852–1964) – formerly Marazion Road
Penzance (1852)

NORTH CORNWALL RAILWAY STATIONS, OPENED IN ABOUT 1890, CLOSED 1967

Launceston
Egloskerry
Tresmeer
Otterham
Camelford
Port Isaac Road
St Kew Highway
Wadebridge
Padstow

A RAILWAY ACCIDENT

On 13 April 1895 the 5.00 p.m. passenger train from Plymouth to Penzance crashed near Doublebois. As it was the holiday season, the main carriages were more than usually full. As it rounded a curve on an embankment near Clinnick viaduct, travelling at over 40mph, the leading engine turned inwards, and dragging down the soil, became partially buried. Simultaneously the second engine was flung on its side, at right angles across both lines. The first coach, consisting of the guard's van and three third-class compartments, was swung around against the overturned engine, completely wrecking it. The rest of the train was brought to a sudden standstill, and the carriages were badly damaged. The drivers of both engines applied the vacuum brakes, but the train continued, ploughing uphill into a cutting with a steep bank rising high on one side and an equally steep embankment on the other, descending into a valley some 200ft deep. The Up and Down lines were completely blocked, and about thirty people including passengers, drivers, stokers and a guard suffered from shock or were injured, four seriously, though fortunately no lives were lost. The driver of the first engine was scalded on the chest, and suffered cuts and bruises, while the other driver was flung into an adjoining field but only slightly hurt, and the stoker fell between the engine and the first carriage. Doctors from Bodmin and Plymouth were on the scene to attend to those who were hurt. Ten years earlier, a driver had been killed in a similar accident at the same spot. The lines were blocked for the rest of the day but had been cleared by early next morning.

A report issued in June concluded that in future two engines should not be allowed on any Down train between Doublebois and Bodmin Road, as it was unsuitable for very fast running, and the line between those points was not constructed for a speed much over 40mph.

CANALS

Bude Canal, 35 miles long, rising from sea level to an altitude of 433ft, was authorised by Act of Parliament in 1774 but construction was delayed by lack of finance, approved again in 1819 and opened in 1823. The main line ran from Bude to a wharf near Launceston, with an easterly branch to Blagdonmoor, near Holsworthy, and a northerly feeder arm from Tamar Lake, Virworthy. It closed in 1891.

Liskeard & Looe Union Canal, 5 miles long, 25 locks, ran from Terras Mill, Looe, to Moorswater near Liskeard, carrying lime and sand, authorised by Act of Parliament in 1825, opened 1828, closed about 1910.

St Columb Canal, sometimes known as Edyvean's Canal, was proposed by engineer John Edyvean and authorised by Act of Parliament in 1773 in order to carry sea sand, seaweed and stone inland from Mawgan Porth. Two sections of the 30-mile route from

Porth to Mawgan Porth via St Columb Major, comprising about 6½ miles, were built and briefly used during the next ten years or so, and part of it may have been briefly used in about 1780. Edyvean had financed the project, but realised that he was unlikely to recoup much of his investment, and no further progress was made. In 1829 the idea of a canal from St Columb to Mawgan Porth was briefly revived but then abandoned.

Parnall Canal, half a mile long, at the Carlaze tin mine near St Austell, including a tunnel into the mine, was built in about 1720 but closed about twelve years later after a tunnel fall rendered it unsafe.

Par Canal, 1 mile long and with three locks, ran from Pontsmill to Par Harbour, St Austell Bay, opened in 1847 and closed in 1873.

TURNPIKE TRUSTS

Until the end of the nineteenth century, highway maintenance was the responsibility of individual parishes. With the growth of industry and the need to transport raw materials and finished goods, increasing traffic required a new means of dealing with the maintenance of roads, resulting in an Act of Parliament in the eighteenth century sanctioning the formation of turnpike trusts which were permitted to build roads and charge tolls. The following trusts were established in Cornwall.

Bodmin, created 1769, 57 miles
Bodmin and Roche, 1836, 11 miles
Callington, 1764, 34 miles
Camelford, Wadebridge and St Columb (Haleworthy), 1760, 36 miles
Creed and St Just, 1762, 18 miles
Hayle Bridge Causeway, 1825, 6 miles
Helston, 1761, 26 miles
Launceston, 1760, 46 miles
Liskeard, 176, 42 miles
Penryn and Redruth, 1763, 8 miles
Penzance to St Just, 1863, 10 miles

Saltash, 1762, 20 miles
St Austell and Lostwithiel, 1761, 18 miles
Trebarwith Sands Road, 1825, 2 miles
Truro, 1754, 56 miles

ROADS

The A30, 284 miles long and sometimes known as the Great South West Road, has trunk road status between Honiton and Penzance. It was the most direct route from London until superseded by the M3 and the A303. In Cornwall it is mostly dual carriageway, with only two short sections of single carriageway, a total of about 20 miles, a 2-mile stretch on Bodmin Moor, and the rest between Carland Cross and Chiverton Cross, near Redruth, a stretch from Treswithian to Ludgvan, and then west of Penzance. The final stretch to Land's End is more rural.

The A39, 204 miles, starts at Bath, goes through Somerset and North Devon to the South Cornwall coast. The section from the North Devon Link Road, Barnstaple to the A30 at Fraddon is known as the Atlantic Highway.

The A38, 292 miles, runs from Bodmin through Dobwalls, Liskeard and over the Tamar Bridge at Saltash all the way to Mansfield, Nottinghamshire. Until the opening of the M5, it was the main south-west holiday route.

Other major roads running between Cornwall and Devon include the A3072 from Hatherleigh and central Devon to Bude, and the A390 from Tavistock to Callington and Liskeard.

John McAdam, the Scottish engineer and road builder who invented 'macadamisation', a hard surface to apply to roads and make them more durable, came to Cornwall in 1798 as a navy victualling officer. He realised that Cornish greenstone would be ideal for the purpose, and the turnpike road from Truro Workhouse to Kiggion, now part of the A39, was the first 'macadam road'.

CORNWALL'S MOTOR HERO

Donald Healey (1898–1988), who was born and died in Perranporth, was a noted automobile engineer, rally driver, and holder of several speed records. In 1931 he won the Monte Carlo rally, driving a 4½-litre Invicta. The same model helped him to victory in the class for unlimited sports cars at the Brighton Speed Trials the next year. In 1945 he formed the Donald Healey Motor Company, which developed the Austin Healey and Austin Healey Sprite.

SHIPWRECKS

The list of shipwrecks off the coast of Cornwall and the Isles of Scilly is inevitably a long one. This one includes the most notable, in chronological order. Figures of fatalities are uncertain in most cases and vary according to source.

Garland, sailing for France with the king's wardrobe, jewellery and other valuables, was driven off course in a storm on 30 January 1649 (the same day that King Charles I was beheaded), with only two survivors out of a crew of 60.

The Isles of Scilly naval disaster, one of the worst in British maritime history, occurred on 22 October 1707 during the War of the Spanish Succession. HMS *Eagle*, HMS *Association*, HMS *Firebrand* and HMS *Romney* were returning from Gibraltar to Portsmouth, but due to a combination of bad weather and navigational errors they sailed off course and ran aground on the rocks at Scilly, with between 1,500 and 2,000 men lost, including Sir Cloudesley Shovell, Commander-in-Chief of the Fleet.

Royal Anne Galley, en route to Barbados, where Lord Belhaven was going to take up the governorship, was forced by bad weather to return to port at Falmouth, and on 10 November 1721 was wrecked on Stag Rocks, off Lizard Point, with the loss of 207 men (including Belhaven) and only three survivors.

Nancy was dashed to pieces off the Isles of Scilly, and sank off the uninhabited island of Rosevear in February 1784. The body of 24-year-old Ann Cargill, actress and opera singer, was recovered from the wreckage a week later, 'floating in her shift', apparently with an infant child at her breast. She had made her stage debut at the age of 11 at Covent Garden. In 1776 she was cast in the lead role of Polly in John Gay's *The Beggar's Opera*. As she was under legal age her father tried to seize her one night on her way to the theatre, but he was restrained by the audience and the performance went ahead. In 1780 she was said to be the world's highest-paid actress, but her affairs and elopements shocked London society. Her lover Captain John Haldane was stationed in Calcutta so she went to join him but the prime minister, William Pitt, declaring that 'an actress should not be defiling the pure shores of India', summoned her home. On their return the *Nancy* was lost, with 36 crew and about twelve other passengers drowned. It was said that she was carrying jewels and cash worth about £200,000 with her, but none were ever found. Cargill was buried at Rosevear Island, but her body was later disinterred and reburied at Old Town Church, St Mary's. It is said that the ghosts of her and her child still haunt Rosevear to this day. In September 2008 it was revealed that two divers, both local historians, had found a cannon and other artefacts from a wreck dating from the correct period near where the *Nancy* supposedly went down. They believed the vessel had sunk on Western Rocks, and that the ship's passengers and crew had taken to a smaller boat which capsized as they were trying to land.

HMS *Anson*, which left Falmouth for Brittany but was forced back by bad weather and overturned off Loe Bar near Porthleven on 29 December 1807, with up to 120 drowned. This was the disaster which inspired inventor Henry Trengrouse (see p. 44) to invent his rocket-powered life-saving apparatus.

HMS *Primrose*, a brig sloop sailing for Spain, ran aground on 22 January 1809 on the Manacles with only one survivor from about 100 on board. That same night *Dispatch*, a transport vessel travelling from Corunna with a detachment of the 7th Hussars returning home after fighting in the Peninsular War, was wrecked at the same place, with 104 drowned and only seven survivors.

Queen, sailing from Lisbon for Portsmouth, was wrecked in a violent storm off Trefusis Point on 14 January 1814, with about 100 survivors out of 300, mostly soldiers, on board.

Cherubim and *Ocean Home*, two American cargo ships, collided off Lizard Point on 5 September 1856, with 77 from both vessels drowned.

Mary Welch, a cargo-carrying schooner-brigantine, bound from Cardiff for Hayle, was wrecked off Godrevy on 20 October 1857 with the loss of all six on board.

Bay of Panama, a cargo-carrying ship, left Calcutta for Dundee on 18 November 1890 and ran aground 4 March 1891 (an exceptionally hard winter) at Nare Point in a violent blizzard. Of the 40 men on board, 23 were either lost overboard or frozen to death.

SS *Mohegan* left Tilbury Docks for New York on 13 October 1898, and ran onto the Manacles next day with 106 out of 150 on board lost.

Peace and Plenty, a Lowestoft fishing smack, capsized in Padstow harbour on the night of 11 April 1900. Although five members of the crew and a boy were saved, three others were lost. Eight members of the lifeboat crew who went to her rescue were also drowned.

HMS *Warwick* was sunk by a U-boat off Trevose Head on 20 February 1944, with 67 killed and 93 survivors. Several British and Allied vessels were torpedoed and sunk off the Cornish coast during the Second World War but with remarkably few casualties.

Solomon Browne, a lifeboat, went to the rescue of Irish-registered coaster *Union Star* on 19 December 1981 in severe weather in Mount's Bay, but both vessels were lost as were the lives of all 16 involved, including eight volunteer lifeboatmen.

Maria Asumpta, a Spanish brig, on her first voyage after a refit at Gloucester, entered Padstow Harbour but foundered after hitting rocks at Rump Point on 30 May 1995. The crew abandoned ship but three were drowned; the captain was later convicted and imprisoned for manslaughter of those who died as a result of 'gross negligence'.

CORNWALL LIGHTHOUSES

Bishop Rock, Isles of Scilly
Godrevy
Gribben Head
Lizard Lighthouse
Longships
Pendeen Lighthouse
Round Island Light, Isles of Scilly
Tater Du Lighthouse
Trevose Head Lighthouse

AIRPORTS

Newquay Cornwall Airport, Mawgan in Pydar, 5 miles north-east of Newquay, is Cornwall's main commercial airport. With a runway of 9,000ft, it was initially built and maintained as a United States Air Force strategic nuclear bomber base. After the end of the Cold War, the United States terminated its involvement with the base. The runway was operated by RAF St Mawgan until December 2008.

Bodmin Airfield
Land's End, St Just
Penzance Heliport
Perranporth Airfield
RNAS Culdrose
St Mary's, Isles of Scilly
Tresco Heliport, Isles of Scilly
Truro Aerodrome

FOOD AND DRINK

Fishing

According to the Objective One Partnership Office, Truro, in 2005, Newlyn was the largest fishing port in England in terms of the value of fish landed (7,500 tons, worth an estimated £17,500,000). The value of the entire fish catching and processing sector was put at £99,000,000, representing employment of over 5,000 people and contributing 2 per cent of the region's GDP. The port handles over forty different species of fish, in addition to lobsters, crabs, crawfish and scallops.

Although the county's pilchard fishing industry days have long since peaked, in 1871 a record amount, over 16,000 tonnes, was exported from Newlyn to Italy.

The Cornish have not surprisingly long been enthusiastic consumers of fish, though some have been known to indulge their appetites a little excessively. According to *The West Briton* of 3 June 1831, 'in a public house at Truro . . . a man actually eat (*sic*) two eels and a plaice, undressed, for a trifling wager. The eels were alive at the time he commenced his brutal feat, and he devoured them, bones, &c., just as they were bought from the market.' He was not the only one. On 5 December 1834, the same paper reported that 'a man named Stephens of St Columb, generally known by the designation of "Daffy Dilly", whilst last week at Newquay, undertook to eat for a wager fifty-two fried pilchards, which feat he accomplished in the space of an hour, to the astonishment of a large assemblage of persons. He afterwards offered to wage that he would in the same space of time eat a moderate size leg of mutton, which proposal no one however seemed inclined to accept.'

The name of Rick Stein has long been synonymous with fish cookery. He was born in Oxfordshire but later moved to Padstow, and opened his first business in the town in 1974. Well known as a TV presenter and author of books on his speciality, he owns four restaurants, a bistro, a café and a seafood delicatessen and patisserie shop. Padstow is so synonymous with his name that it is sometimes jocularly known as 'Padstein'.

PASTIES

The Cornish pasty is said to date back to the late eighteenth century. It was initially made to cater for the large appetites of working men, especially miners, and contained meat and vegetables at one end, apples and cream at the other. The miner's initial was sometimes added on the far right-hand corner, so the man for whom it had been made could confidently put it down half-eaten beside the others during his shift and be sure of picking the right one up again later, always assuming he was careful not to eat the wrong end first.

Ginsters, based in Callington, is the biggest-selling pasty maker in Britain. The business began in the 1960s when farmer Geoffrey Ginster, who ran an egg-packing station employing 30 people, launched a service selling fresh pasties to local retailers by van. An instant success, it soon expanded until it was employing 700 people. In 1977 it was sold to Leicester-based Samworth Brothers.

Warrens Bakery, a family-owned chain based in St Just in Penwith, is perhaps the next best-known maker of Cornish pasties, and also Cornish saffron cake, with over 50 shops in the south-west. Founded in 1860, it also supplies pasties to Fortnum & Mason.

PIES

Stargazy pie is a traditional Cornish dish made with baked pilchards, eggs and potatoes, covered with a pastry crust. The heads and sometimes tails protrude through the crust, gazing upwards at the stars, hence the name. Originating from Mousehole, it is traditionally eaten during the festival of Tom Bawcock's Eve, 23 December. Bawcock is said to be a sixteenth-century fisherman who made a particularly magnificent catch during a stormy winter, though there is some doubt as to whether such a character ever existed. The tale forms the basis of *The Mousehole Cat* (1991), a children's book by Antonia Barber, which tells of Bawcock and his cat Mowzer who go fishing during the storm.

CHEESES

Cornwall makes about 10 per cent of all recognised British varieties. The main companies are:

Cornish Cheese Company, Liskeard: Cornish Blue, Beast of Bodmin, Cornish Camembert, Farmhouse Cornish brie

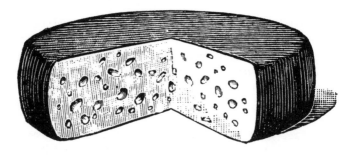

Cornish Country Larder, Newquay: Cornish Brie, Chatel, Cornish Organic Brie, Cornish Smokey, St Anthony, West Country Cornish brie, St Endelion, Village Green, Gevrick Goats Cheese

Lynher Dairies, Ponsanooth, Truro: Cornish Yarg, Cornish Tiskey, Cornish Black Pepper, Cornish Garland, Cornish Herb and Garlic, Cornish Tarragon, Stithians Special

Menallack Farm, Penryn: Tala, Nanterrow, Nanterrow Chives & Garlic, Buffalo Soft, Cheethams Chough, Cornish Feta, Cornish Herb Whirl, Cornish Smoke, Fingals, Garden of Eden, Heligan, Menallack Farmhouse Semi Hard, Menallack Chives & Garlic, Mrs Finn, Polmesk, St Erme, St Laudus, St Piran, Treverva Green, Vintage Farmhouse, Vithen

Whalesborough Farm Foods, Bude: Cornish Herbert, Keltic Gold, Miss Muffet, Trelawney

Cornish Cuisine, Penryn: Cornish Smoked Cheddar, St Agnes Brie, Tesyn, Tintagel Organic, Tresco, Trevellas

Dairy Crest, Davidstow: Cathedral City, Davidstow

Neet Foods, Bude: St Marwenne

POTATOES AND
DAIRY PRODUCTS

In 1847 a Cornish potato famine, coincidentally not long after the catastrophic one in Ireland, was followed by a large increase in wheat and flour prices. The result was to put the price of bread beyond Cornish miners and their families, with subsequent unrest known to posterity as the 'Corn riots'. In May and June 1847 there were disturbances at Wadebridge, Redruth and Penzance, where flour warehouses and markets were robbed and pillaged.

The wet Cornish climate and poor soil are particularly suitable for growing rich grass required for dairying, hence the production of Cornish clotted cream, ice cream and fudge. In 2010 the county had 896 dairy farms, with 73,000 cows producing between them over 500,000,000 litres of milk annually.

BREWERIES

St Austell Brewery (founded 1851): Tribute, Proper Job, Black Prince, Trelawney Ale

Skinners Brewing Co, Newham, Truro (1997): Cornish Knocker, Heligan Honey, Spriggan Ale, Betty Stogs, Ginger Tosser, Keel Over, Hunny Bunny

Sharp's Brewery, Wadebridge (1994): Doom Bar, Chalky's Bark, Cornish Coaster, Sharp's Special, Sharp's Own, Chalky's Bite

Wooden Hand Brewery, Truro (2004): Cornish Mutiny, Black Pearl, Cornish Buccaneer, Cornish Mutiny, Cornish Steam Lager

Keltek Brewery, Redruth: Magik, Golden Lance, King, Even Keel

Spingo, named after the Old English for strong beer, is the general name for various beers brewed at the fifteenth-century Blue Anchor Inn, Helston. Originally a monk's rest house, producing honey-based mead, after the dissolution of the monasteries it became an inn and began brewing its own spingo, which comes in three strengths. It is thought to be the oldest private brewery in the country still in existence.

The inn, where miners generally gathered to collect their wages, has an interesting tale or two to tell. In 1717 the landlord unwisely allowed himself to become involved in an argument and received a fatal stab wound. Seventy-four years later another landlord, Jimmy James, was likewise involved in an altercation in the bar and stabbed to death in the head with a bayonet. The two soldiers responsible, Ben Willoughby and John Taylor, were hanged. The trail of death continued in 1828 when a man fell to his death in the well, and in 1849 when another landlord, James Judd, hanged himself in the skittle alley.

Sotweed, the Elizabethan name for tobacco, was said to have been introduced into England from Virginia by Sir Walter Raleigh, who first smoked it in public as a guest of the Killigrew family in Falmouth in 1586. This is disputed by those who claim that the habit had been brought from France to England, although it is arguable that Raleigh was the first well-known person to do so. At any rate he is the one most widely blamed for leading people astray.

HOTELS, CLUBS AND PUBS WITH CELEBRITY CONNECTIONS

Old Ferry Inn, Bodinnick

Daphne Du Maurier and her family came here for lunch in 1926 when they moved from London to Fowey, the start of the author's lifelong love affair with the county.

Jamaica Inn, Bolventor

An eighteenth-century inn built to provide food and shelter to travellers on Bodmin Moor, and the inspiration for Daphne Du Maurier's novel of the same title. It was bought by thriller writer Alistair Maclean in 1964, but he only stayed there briefly and left the running of the business to his brother.

Ship Inn, East Looe

Wilkie Collins was on a walking tour of Cornwall in 1850 with his friend Harry Brandling, when they stopped here overnight. They likewise stayed at several other inns, including the Ship Inn, East Fowey; the First & Last, Land's End; the Red Lion, St Columb; the Royal Talbot, Lostwithiel; and the Union Hotel, Penzance. He published his peripatetic reminiscences the following year in *Rambles Beyond Railways*.

Shades Nightclub, formerly Pedros, Falmouth

Owned in the late 1960s and early '70s by choreographer and TV presenter Lionel Blair.

Old Inn, Mullion

Robert Francis Kilvert, clergyman and diarist, visited and left an entry in his diary, 22 July 1870, in which he noted the welcome he received from landlady Mary Mundy, 'a genuine Cornish Celt, impulsive, warm-hearted, excitable, demonstrative, imaginative and eloquent. We went into a sitting room upstairs, unpacked the hampers, and ordered dinner to be ready when we came back in an hour's time.'

Dinah Maria Craik, novelist and poet, stayed here on holiday with her two young nieces in 1883, and left her impressions in *An Unsentimental Journey Through Cornwall* of being greeted at the door by the landlady, possibly Mrs Mundy again, 'a bright, brown-faced little woman with the reddest of cheeks and the blackest of eyes.' She showed them into a parlour at the back, where they were thrilled to see spread out for them 'not one of your dainty afternoon teas, with two or three wafery slices of bread and butter, but a regular substantial meal' accompanied by candles, which revealed the bright teapot, and 'the gigantic home-baked loaf, which it seemed sacrilegious to have turned into toast.'

A later visitor was the engineer and inventor Guglielmo Marconi, who stopped here in 1903 when coming to Cornwall as the first transatlantic wireless message was transmitted from Newfoundland to Poldhu.

Abbey Hotel, Penzance

Owned by Jean Shrimpton, model and actress, during the 1960s.

WHAT'S IN A (PUB) NAME?

The Finnygook, Crafthole

The gook, or ghost, of a smuggler killed while trying to escape capture by coastguards is said to haunt the area nearby.

The Bucket of Blood, Phillack

A landlord once went to the well for a bucket of water but only found blood there instead. Close examination revealed a recently mutilated body at the bottom. In any list of strange British pub names, this generally comes near the top.

The Bettle and Chisel, Delabole

Tools used for splitting slate, an appropriate name for a hostelry close to one of the world's largest slate quarries.

TIN AND COPPER MINING

Tin and copper mining in Cornwall date back to about 2100 BC, when the county was said to have been visited by metal traders from the eastern Mediterranean. Cornwall and west Devon provided most of

Britain's tin, copper and also arsenic. At its height in the early nineteenth century, the Cornish Tin Mining Industry had about 600 steam engines in use, but from the mid-nineteenth century the industry was in decline. South Crofty, near Camborne, the last working tin mine in Europe, closed in March 1998.

The first Stannary Cornish Charter was issued in 1201 by King John. The county was divided into four districts, and within these the crown designated certain towns as coinage towns. Four times a year all tin mined in Cornwall had to be taken there for assaying prior to sale. The tin ingot was weighed and coined, and a small corner was removed from the ingot so it could be analysed for any possible impurities.

The county's worst mining disaster was at East Wheal Rose near Newquay on 9 July 1846, when 39 men were killed after the mine flooded during a heavy thunderstorm and torrential rain. A marginally less severe tragedy occurred on 20 October 1919 at Levant Mine, when an engine collapsed after a bolt sheared off, and 31 men and boys lost their lives.

The county's deepest mine (and for some years said to be the deepest mine in the world) was Dolcoath, over 3,100ft, hence the old Cornish expression 'deep as Dolcoath'. It closed in 1921.

CHINA CLAY

The china clay or kaolin deposits in Cornwall, the largest in the world, have been worked since their discovery by Quaker apothecary-cum-potter William Cookworthy at Tregonning Hill in 1746. Kaolin is basically highly decomposed granite, rotted by the prolonged soaking of water. Although the substance had been used by the Chinese many centuries earlier to manufacture a pure white porcelain, prior to discoveries of a few deposits in parts of Europe and America early in the eighteenth century, this was the first time it had been found in Britain, and the quality was much better than the others, as well as vastly superior to the earthenware and stoneware previously used for English pottery. By 1768 Cookworthy had patented a way to use the clay, and developed a porcelain factory at Plymouth.

Other potteries soon began to use Cornish china clay, with most of the pottery factories owning rights to mine the material themselves, and kaolin was later used as a whitener by the paper industry. By 1910 production was almost one million tons a year. Cornwall held a near-monopoly of kaolin on world markets, with 75 per cent of output exported chiefly to North America and Europe.

In 1919 the three largest producers, West of England China Clay Co., Martyn Brothers and North Cornwall China Clays, which between them accounted for around half the industry's capacity, merged to form English China Clays (ECC), which merged with its two major rivals, John Lovering and H.D. Pochin in 1932, forming English Clays, Lovering, Pochin, & Co. (ECLP). In 1956 when the Lovering and Pochin families were bought out, the company became ECC International Ltd. This was acquired in 1999 for £756,000,000 by the French company Imetal which then became Imerys.

80 per cent of the present output of china clay produced is used in the manufacture of paper, with 12 per cent in the ceramics industry and the remaining 8 per cent in products including paint, rubber, plastics, pharmaceuticals, cork, cosmetics and agricultural products.

The port of Charlestown with its single dock secured much of the clay shipping trade. One of the largest clay pits, near St Austell, has since been used for the construction of the Eden Project (see p. 83).

OTHER SUBSTANCES

Granite, lead, zinc and silver have also been mined extensively in the county. In 1902 a block of granite was moved from the Polkanugga Quarry. Weighing 2,738 tons, it took 110lb of black powder to shift it, and at that time it held the world record for the largest single block ever dislodged in one piece until 1930.

CORNWALL'S TOP 20 TOWNS BY POPULATION

According to data from the Office for National Statistics in 2007, the following towns are the most heavily populated in Cornwall.

1. Camborne-Redruth
2. St Austell
3. Truro
4. Falmouth
5. Newquay
6. Penzance
7. Saltash
8. Bodmin
9. Helston
10. St Blazey-Par
11. St Ives
12. Liskeard
13. Launceston
14. Torpoint
15. Penryn
16. Hayle
17. Bude-Stratton
18. Wadebridge
19. Callington
20. Looe

54 per cent of the county's population live in the above towns, and 30 per cent of these in the six largest towns.

Cornwall's only city, Truro, was granted city status by Queen Victoria in 1877. Although not the largest by population, it has long been the county's administrative centre.

At the time of writing, according to the latest available population estimates from Cornwall County Council, mid-2010, there are an estimated 535,300 people resident in the county, an increase of 4,200 on the previous year.

Charles Abbot, MP for Helston from 1795 to 1802, was largely responsible for the passing of the 1800 Census Act, leading to the first regular census of the population of Britain the following year.

PORT QUIN – THE VANISHING VILLAGE

Towns usually develop from small settlements, which grow into villages – and then keep on growing. Only rarely do they disappear off the face of the earth altogether. However, the county can lay claim to one which did – the fishing village of Port Quin, about 2 miles from Port Isaac, the Cornish 'village that died'.

One night, probably early in the nineteenth century, the total population suddenly disappeared. Several different theories have been offered. It was thought that the village may have been smitten by a sudden epidemic, after which the survivors buried their dead and dispersed elsewhere, before news of the illness had a chance to spread and result in them being ostracised by those in neighbouring communities. Another possibility was that a ship got into difficulties on the rocks near the end of the inlet into the village during a heavy gale, and that all the local men who tried to help in the rescue were lost together with their boats.

A separate explanation suggests that the entire male population were drowned one particularly stormy night in or around 1698 while they were out fishing, and as the women could not continue to live there on their own, they decided to go elsewhere. Yet another theory has it that the village had been heavily dependent on the proceeds of smuggling at the end of the eighteenth century, and somebody had received due warning that a raid by Customs & Excise could be expected very soon, so everybody fled before the long arm of the law could catch up with them.

The most credible and generally accepted explanation was that the herring and pilchard fishing on which the village depended gradually declined, the local mines closed down, and people simply moved away.

Nevertheless it was said that when the last survivors departed, they left food on the tables, and went with the rooms still furnished, yet made no effort to take their clothes or other personal possessions with them. It was as if every family had been summoned outside for a temporary evacuation and expected they would return within minutes as if nothing had happened.

8

RELIGION, WARS & FOLKLORE

CORNWALL CHURCHES

Cathedral of the Blessed Virgin Mary, Truro

Cornwall's only cathedral was built between 1880 and 1887, apart from the western steeples which were completed in 1910. 300ft long, with a central tower 250ft high, it lies on the site of the old parish church, the fifteenth-century south aisle of which was incorporated into the new building. Designed by Gothic Revival architect John Pearson, it is one of only three cathedrals in Britain with three spires, the others being in Edinburgh and Lichfield.

St Protus and St Hyacinth, Blisland

Built on the edge of a village green, sometimes erroneously said to be the only village in the county to have one, this mainly Norman church was transformed in the fifteenth century by a tower of large blocks of local granite, as well as a porch, south aisle, and south and north transepts. It is notable for its barrel roofs with carved angels and bosses. Major restoration was undertaken in the late nineteenth century.

St Breage, Breage

A fifteenth-century granite church, with a nave and chancel, both with aisles, and two short battlemented transepts. It is particularly notable for wall paintings in which the medieval colours of red, blue and gold, rediscovered in the late nineteenth century, have survived intact.

Cubert (formerly St Cubert's Church), Cubert

A fourteenth-century church, enlarged by a south aisle a century later, with a pillared Norman granite font.

St Winwalloe, Gunwalloe

A mainly fifteenth-century church, set behind a small headland, with a detached tower set into the headland rock, Norman font and wagon roof, or barrel vault roof design, over the south aisle.

St James the Great, Kilkhampton

Largely rebuilt in the fifteenth century, though some of it is believed to date back to the tenth or eleventh century, being one of several churches dedicated to St James on a pilgrims' route which eventually leads to Santiago de Compostela in northern Spain. It has a spectacular Norman south doorway and buttressed Perpendicular tower of eight bells.

St Sidwell, Laneast

Thirteenth-century cruciform church enlarged two centuries later, when the south aisle and tower were completed and the church was embellished with woodwork and glass. A major restoration took place in 1848.

St Willow, Lanteglos by Fowey

A mostly late fourteenth-century church, particularly the masonry over the main doorway, though extensively restored in the early twentieth century. The thirteenth-century octagonal font is carved from Norman stone, and it also has a plaque on the wall presented to the parish by Charles II in 1668 in recognition of its loyalty to the royal cause during the Civil War.

St Swithin, Launcells

Once described by John Betjeman as 'the least spoilt church in Cornwall', its carved benches are regarded as among the county's finest.

The three barrel roofs are supported by ten arches, the floor is paved with medieval encaustic tiles, and the rood loft stairs have been left uncovered.

St Mary Magdalene, Launceston

Financed by Sir Henry Trecarrel, a local lord of the manor, and completed in 1542, this granite church includes a chancel, nave, north and south aisles and eight arches. The interior carving of the roof, the work of one man, includes 162 angels and 400 bosses, and it is also noted for its intricately carved granite exterior around three sides of the building. The detached tower, built in about 1380, 84ft high, contains six bells and a clock.

St Melor, Linkinhorne

Built in the sixteenth century, it stands on the site of a smaller probably fourteenth-century church, and retains the Norman south aisle and font. It includes fourteenth-century paintings, a fine Elizabethan table used as a side chapel altar, and Elizabethan pews. The square tower, 120ft high, and the north side were refurbished in 1891.

St Bartholomew, Lostwithiel

Mainly fourteenth-century, it includes a thirteenth-century tower, and an octagonal spire added early the following century. The east window of five lights, 30ft high, is considered one of the county's finest.

St Madrona (or Madron), Madron

Fifteenth-century church with wagon roofs, embellished with about 200 bosses, and a Norman font. Before it was completed the vicar, Benedict Tregos, had lent his support to the Yorkist pretender Perkin Warbeck, and in order to avoid being charged with treason by Henry VII, he paid for the north aisle himself, had decoration of Tudor roses added, and the royal arms on expensive panelling.

St Morwenna and John the Baptist, Morwenstow

Although Norman, it probably replaced an earlier Saxon church on the same site, with additions made in the thirteenth, fifteenth and sixteenth centuries, and was extensively restored in the nineteenth century with slate roofs during Parson Hawker's time. The church and porch doorways consist of parts of a Norman doorway from another presumably long-demolished church. Morwenstow is the most northerly parish in Cornwall.

St Mellanus, Mullion

Fifteenth-century church, although founded about two centuries earlier and retaining the original octagonal font. It was extensively rebuilt and is noted for the striking carved original fifteenth-century benches. It was restored in the twentieth century with fine fan vaulting and panelled loft, and the roof was rebuilt in 1988.

St Newelina, Newlyn East

Norman church rededicated in 1259, most of the present structure is from the fourteenth and fifteenth centuries. The south arcade of six bays and font are from the Norman period, while the carved, painted and gilded ribs and carved choir stalls are medieval.

St Paul, Paul

Mainly fifteenth-century in origin, the 89ft tower is one of the tallest in the county, probably having been intended partly as a seamark for ships. It suffered major damage during a Spanish raid in 1595, with only the tower, south porch and part of the western end surviving. The churchyard contains a memorial to noted Cornish-speaker Dolly Pentreath, placed there in 1860 by Lucien Bonaparte, nephew of Napoleon.

All Saints, Pentewan

Built in 1821, All Saints includes several Tudor and Jacobean windows from the ruins of Polrudden Manor. It was for some years closed as a place of worship and used as a carpenter's workshop, but reopened as a church in 1878.

St Probus and St Grace, Probus

Probaby Norman, built on the site of a former Celtic monastery on which King Athelstan later founded a church in AD 930. The sixteenth-century tower, at 129ft high, is the tallest in the county, and it is also noted for its fine canopied niches and belfry windows. It was extensively restored in 1851 with various additions made later in the nineteenth century.

St Anthony, St Anthony-in-Meneage

Thirteenth-century, built on a rock by Helford River. The fifteenth-century granite tower has a modern door incorporating a latchet door for dogs, and also allowing hens to roost in the belfry.

Holy Trinity, St Austell

Originally built in about 1169 from Pentewan stone and dedicated to St Austolus, the oldest surviving part is the chapel south of the chancel, while the tower is fifteenth-century. The whole building was restored in the nineteenth century.

St Germanus, St Germans

Formerly the site of the Saxon Cathedral for Cornwall and then an Augustinian monastery, it was rebuilt in about 1160–70, and rebuilt again to become a church. At the time of the dissolution of the monasteries, it was stripped of everything of value and then became a private residence before reverting to use as a church.

St Justus, St Just-in-Roseland

Said to be the county's most photographed church, it has a spectacular waterside setting, surrounded by tropical trees and plants. According to legend, this was where Jesus landed when brought to Cornwall by Joseph of Arimathea. Built on the site of a fifth-century chapel, it is mainly thirteenth-century, and noted for its seven granite bays. In the will of John Randall, a local squire who died on 23 July 1733, a sum of 10s was bequeathed for the rector to preach a funeral sermon every year on the anniversary for the next thousand years.

St Winnow, near Lostwithiel

Although of Norman foundation, built on the site of the seventh-century oratory of St Winnoc, most of it dates from the fifteenth century, when the south wall was demolished and the south aisle, arcade and roofs were built. It has one of the county's few surviving Elizabethan pulpits, as well as carved bench ends including a St Catherine's Wheel, and a man dressed in a Cornish kilt who is drinking cider.

MONASTIC HOUSES IN CORNWALL

Altarnun Monastery, in existence before 1066 – no further details known

Bodmin Abbey of St Mary & St Petroc (Augustinian Canons Regular), founded 1881, raised to Abbey status 1953

Bodmin Greyfriars (Franciscan Friars Minor, Conventual), founded before 1260, dissolved 1538

Bodmin Priory (successively Celtic monks, Benedictine monks, Augustinian Canons Regular), founded in the sixth century by St Petroc, dissolved 1539

Breage Grange (Cistercian monks) – no further details

Cardinham Grange, founded probably in the eleventh century, dissolved in about 1536

Constantine Monastery – no further details

Crantock, St Carrock's or St Karentoc's Monastery (secular canons collegiate), founded before 1066, dissolved 1549

Gulval, Dingerein or Dinurrin Monastery, near Penzance (Celtic monks), founded by St Gudwall – no further details

Kea Monastery (Celtic monks), in existence during the eleventh century – no further details

Lammana Priory, Looe Island (Benedictine monks), founded in the sixth century, later chantry chapel of Dawnay family, dissolved 1329

Lansallos Monastery (Celtic monks) – no further details

Lannachebran Cell, St Keverne (Cistercian monks), founded in the sixth century under the tutelage of St Achebran, dissolved 1527

Launcells Priory, near Stratton (Celtic monks), probably dissolved in the eleventh century

Launceston Priory (Augustinian Canons Regular), founded in 1127, dissolved in 1539, restored 1871 and now in parochial use as Church of St Thomas the Apostle. There had been another Launceston priory on another site nearby, founded in the early ninth century

Lanwethinoc Monastery, Padstow (Celtic monks), founded by Bishop Wethinoc – no further details

Madron Monastery (Celtic monks), probably dissolved by the twelfth century

Manaccan Monastery, The Lizard (Celtic monks)

Mawgan in Pydar Franciscan Monastery, or Franciscan Monastery of St Joseph and St Anne (Franciscan monks) – no further details

Minster Priory, Forrabury and Minster (Celtic monks), founded in the eleventh century by William de Bottreaux, dissolved probably early fifteenth century

Paul Grange (Cistercian monks), founded in about 1300, date of dissolution unknown

Probus Monastery (Celtic monks, then secular canons collegiate), founded 924 probably by King Athelstan, dissolved 1549

Rialton Grange, St Columb Minor (Augustinian Canons Regular), probably dissolved by fifteenth century

St Anthony's Monastery, St Anthony-in-Meneage (Celtic monks, later Benedictine monks), founded probably in the eleventh century, dissolved after 1381

St Anthony-in-Roseland Priory (Augustinian Canons Regular), founded before 1288, dissolved 1538

St Buryan's Monastery (Celtic monks), founded in about 930 probably by King Athelstan, dissolved 1545

St Carrok's Monastery, St Winnow (Celtic monks, later Cluniac monks), founded in about 1100, dissolved 1537

St German's Priory (Celtic monks, later Augustinian Canons Regular), founded in abour 930, dissolved 1539

St Goran's Monastery (Celtic monks), founded sixth century, dissolved in about 1280

St Kew Cell (Augustinian monks, later Augustinian secular canons), founded sixth century, date of dissolution unknown

St Matthew's Monastery – no further details

St Mawgan Monastery, or Lanherne Monastery, St Mawgan in Pydar (Celtic monks, then Cluniac monks), dissolved probably in the late eleventh century, Carmelite convent later built on site

St Michael's Mount Priory (Benedictine monks), founded probably in the eighth century, seized during Hundred Years' War, 1362, dissolved in about 1414

St Neot's Monastery (Celtic monks), founded in the sixth century, dissolved after 1084

St Piran's Monastery, Perranzabuloe (Celtic monks), founded in the sixth century, dissolved in about 1085

Saltash Abbey – no further details

Scilly Priory, Tresco (Celtic monks, then Benedictine monks), founded in about 964, dissolved in about 1538

Sclerder Abbey, near Looe (successively Dames de la Retraite, Franciscan Recollects, Carmelite nuns, Sisters of the Sacred Hearts of Jesus and Mary, Minoresses, Franciscan nuns, Carmelite nuns), founded 1843

Temple Templars Preceptory, Temple, near Blisland (Knights Templar), founded twelfth century, dissolved 1308–12

Tintagel Monastery, thought to have been a Celtic institution founded in fourth century, later became the site of Tintagel Castle

Trebeign (Treleigh, Turleigh) Preceptory, (Knights Templar, then Knights Hospitaller), founded before 1199, dissolved in about 1557

Tregonan Cell, St Ewe (Celtic monks), founded in the sixth century but dissolved by the eleventh century

Tregonan Grange, or St Keverne Grange (Cistercian monks), founded before 1263, dissolved by 1527

Tregony Priory (Augustinian Canons Regular), founded in about 1100, thought to have been dissolved in the thirteenth century, with no ruins remaining

Truro Convent of the Epiphany (Sisterhood of the Epiphany), founded 1883 by George Wilkinson, Bishop of Truro in Tregolls Road, moved a century later to Copeland Court, which was renamed Epiphany House

Truro Blackfriars (Dominican Friars), founded in about 1240 by Reskiner family, dissolved 1538

Tywardreath Priory (Benedictine monks), St Andrew, founded in about 1088, probably by Richard FitzTurold, Lord of Cardinham Castle, dissolved 1536

SAINTS

The following all have some Cornish connection, some less tenuous than others. St Piran is regarded as the patron saint of Cornwall, although not without competition from St Petroc and St Michael. What little is known about them is often clouded by legend and varies from source to source.

St Austell

Also St Austol or Austolus, a sixth-century holy man who spent most of his life in Brittany, where he helped to found the Abbey of St Meen with his godfather St Meven. The parish and town of St Austell were named after him. Feast day – the Thursday of Whitsun week.

St Blaise

A physician, bishop of Sebastea (now Sivas), Turkey, who is said to have landed at Par and spent some time in Cornwall, he lived in a cave and cured sick and injured animals. Captured because of his Christian beliefs, he was tortured and beheaded in AD 316. St Blazey is named after him, and the parish church is dedicated to his memory. Feast day – 3 February.

St Breage

Said to be an Irish nun from a Kildare oratory of the fifth or sixth century, though maybe one of several obscure saints to whom a fabricated Irish connection has been attributed, she reputedly travelled to Cornwall with seven other saints to settle at Reyver, near the River Hayle, travelling through the county and founding a church at Chynoweth. St Breage and the village church are named after her. Feast day – formerly 1 May, now 4 June.

St Brioc

Also St Brieuc, Breock or Briavel, a sixth-century Welshman who became the first Abbot of St Briac in Brittany, where he settled and eventually died. He also spent some time in Cornwall where he founded St Breock's Church. Feast day – 17 June or 2 July.

St Budoc

Also St Budeaux or Beuzec, Bishop of Dol in Brittany, believed to have dedicated the parish church of Budock Water around AD 470. Feast day – 8 December.

St Buriana

A sixth-century Irish saint, daughter of an Irish king, who sailed to Cornwall to convert the people there to Christianity and later lived as a hermit at St Buryan. Feast day – 1 May.

St Carantoc

Also St Carantock, Carannog, Cairnech or Karanteg, a sixth-century confessor and abbot who was believed to have preached in Cornwall and built the church bearing his name at Crantock. Feast day – 16 May.

St Constantine

Thought to have been a minor king who renounced his crown to lead the life of a monk, giving his name to the Cornish parish, later village, and bay.

St Cuby

Said to have been the son of Salomon, a King of Cornwall around the sixth century, he went on a pilgrimage to Rome and Jerusalem, was consecrated as a bishop, returned home to find he had succeeded his late father as king, but refused the crown and travelled through the county, founding churches at Duloe, Tregony, Cubert and Landulph, later going to Wales and Ireland. Feast day – 13 August in Cornwall, 8 November elsewhere.

St Endelienta

Also St Endellient or Endellion, thought to be a daughter of the Welsh King Brychan and goddaughter of King Arthur in the fifth and sixth centuries, who travelled from South Wales to Cornwall with her family to convert the people to Christianity. She lived off the milk of a cow while a hermit in a cave at Trentinney. Her shrine was at the church of

St Endellion around which the village of the same name grew up. Feast day – 29 April.

St Erth

Also St Erc or Ercus, the brother of Saints Ia and Uny, who left Ireland for Cornwall, where he founded the church of St Erth around which the village developed. Feast day – 31 October.

St Felec

Also St Felix, a fifth- or sixth-century Christian who was able to converse with cats and lions, and to whom a church at Phillack near Hayle was dedicated. Feast day – 20 November.

St Gwinear

Born in Ireland and converted to Christianity by St Patrick, then went to Brittany and later Cornwall where he was martyred by King Teudar.

St Ia

Also St Hia, Hya or Ives, was an Irish princess, the sister of St Erc, and came as a missionary to Cornwall, joining Saints Fingar and Piala. She was martyred on the River Hayle and buried at St Ives, where the church was erected over her grave and the town gradually developed. Feast day – 3 February.

St Kea

Also St Ke, a late fifth-century saint from northern England or possibly Scotland who had been a bishop in the north before coming to Wales and then Cornwall, where Kea was named after him. He sheltered a deer which was being hunted by the Cornish King Teudar, and had his oxen confiscated. Later he went to Brittany, where he died. Feast day – 5 November.

St Keyne

Also St Cain, Cenau, Cenedion, Ceinwen, Keane, Keyna, or Kayane, a late fifth-century lady from the area between Looe and Liskeard, said to be a dragon slayer and to have given her name to a church and a well, of which the waters will give the upper hand during a marriage to whichever of the newly-wedded couple drinks of them first. Feast day – 8 October.

St Levan

Also St Solomon, Selevan, Selus or Selyf, a late fifth-century warrior prince who may have been one of the early Kings of Cornwall. A stone at St Just in Penwith parish church inscribed 'Selus lies here' is thought to be his memorial.

St Mabyn

Also St Mabena or Mabon, a fifth-century saint thought to be one of the children of Brychan, King of Brycheiniog in Wales. The village and civil parish of St Mabyn are named after her. Feast day – 18 November.

St Materiana

Also St Madrun, Madryn, Merthiana, Mertheriana, or Marcelliana, a fifth-century saint and daughter of King Vortimer. The church of St Materiana, Boscastle, is dedicated to her, and Tintagel parish church contains a statue in the chancel and a stained glass window in the nave, both of her image. Feast day – 19 October.

St Melor

Also St Mylor. A Breton saint, at the age of seven he was savagely attacked by his uncle Riwal, who killed his father and attempted to murder him as well but was dissuaded by a council of bishops, so instead he cut the boy's right hand and left foot off. Both were replaced with artificial limbs made from metal. He was killed seven years later on Riwal's orders. His cult spread from Brittany to Cornwall, with churches dedicated to him at Mylor and Linkinhorne. Feast day – 1 October.

St Meriasek

A fourth-century saint, he was the son of a King of Brittany who became a priest, performed miraculous cures particularly on the disabled and on lepers, and came to Cornwall where he founded an oratory. He is the patron saint of Camborne, where there is a sacred well in his memory thought to have the power of healing the insane. Feast day – alternately 7 June, or the first Friday in the month.

St Morwenna

A sixth-century saint from Morwenstow, and daughter of King Brychan of Brycheiniog, a small independent kingdom in South Wales. She settled at Morwenstow, where there is a parish church dedicated to her and a holy well beyond the cliffs.

St Nectan

A sixth-century saint who lived mostly at Hartland, Devon, he was the eldest child of King Brychan of Brycheiniog. He spent some time at Tintagel as a hermit, and would help swineherds to find missing or strayed animals. One gave him two cows as a reward, and when thieves stole them he tried to convert them to Christianity, but they attacked him and beheaded him in about AD 510. Wherever his blood fell on the soil, foxgloves would grow. A medieval chapel at St Nectan near St Winnow is dedicated to him. Feast day – 17 June, although sometimes observed on 14 February, 18 May, and 4 December.

St Petroc

Also St Petrock, Pedrog, Petrocus or Perreux, he was born in Wales. The son of King Glywys, he came to Cornwall to convert people to Christianity and founded monasteries at Lanwethinoc (which later became Petrocstowe, or Petroc's Place, and subsequently Padstow) and Bodmin. He died in AD 564, while travelling to Lanwethinoc and staying at a farm near Little Petherick. His relics were kept at the monastery but later transferred to Bodmin. There are five churches in Cornwall named after him, rather fewer than in Devon, where he was also active. His major shrine is at St Petroc's Church, Bodmin. He is sometimes known as the captain of Cornish saints. Feast day – 4 June.

St Piran

Also St Peran or Ciaran, an early sixth-century abbot and saint, probably of Irish origin. He was captured by Irish pagans, jealous of his healing powers, tied to a millstone and rolled over the edge of the cliffs into a rough sea which suddenly became calm enough for him to float on the water. After a safe journey he landed on the beach at Perranzabuloe where he was joined by some of his coverts to

Christianity and they founded an abbey at Lanpiran, where he became the abbot. He rediscovered the lost art of tin-smelting which had been practiced in the county in pre-Roman days, and is therefore regarded as the patron saint of tin miners as well as of the county. He was buried at Perranzabuloe, but his remains were later exhumed and some were sent to different reliquaries in the county. The churches at Perranuthnoe and Perranarworthal were dedicated to him, and he gave his name to holy wells at Perranwell and Probus. His feast day, 5 March, is celebrated as the equivalent of a national day for Cornwall.

St Rumon

Also St Rumonus, Ruan, Ronan or Ruadan, an Irish missionary to whom churches at Ruan Lanihorne, Ruan Major and Ruan Minor were dedicated. Feast day – 28 August.

St Sennen

A martyred saint about whom little if anything is known. St Sennen's Church, Sennen, is dedicated to him.

St Tallanus

A religious hermit of the fifth century who lived at Talland near Polperro, and after whom the church at Talland is named.

St Wenna

A Cornish Queen, born in AD 472, died 544. She married King Salomon and founded a church at Morval. She is sometimes confused with another St Wenna, born about AD 463, who converted many people to Christianity in North Cornwall, and founded churches at Talgarth, St Wenn and a chapel at St Kew.

St Winwaloe

The son of Prince Fracan who had fled to Brittany during an epidemic of plague, he was born in about AD 460 and died at his monastery in about 530. He is the patron of churches at Tremaine, Gunwalloe and Landewednack.

ST WINWALOE'S CHURCH AND
THE PENFOUND FAMILY

The Church of St Winwaloe, in the parish of Poundstock, near Widemouth Bay, has had an unfortunate history. During the fourteenth century there was fierce rivalry between a gang of robbers and pirates, who regularly attacked ships sailing off the bay. The Revd William Penfound, who was believed to be a member or at least a close associate of the pirates, fell foul of the robbers. In 1357 several of them burst in on him while he was officiating at a service in the church, and hacked him to death at the altar. Ever since, it is said, his ghost has haunted the building. Not long afterwards another vicar was sentenced to life imprisonment for his part in a murder, and in the sixteenth century another was hanged for leading a rebellion against the changes being made in the *Book of Common Prayer*.

Two more members of the Penfound family, who lived at Penfound Manor, came to a tragic end during the Civil War. The family were staunch Royalists and Kate, one of the daughters, tried to elope with John Trebarfoot of Trebarfoot Manor. As the latter were Parliamentarians, she knew her father Arthur would never agree to their relationship. One evening she climbed down a ladder from her bedroom window to the courtyard, where John was waiting for her. Arthur Penfound was lying in wait for them, and he tried to prevent them from leaving. Swords were drawn and in the ensuing struggle, John Trebarfoot was killed, while father and daughter both later died from their wounds.

QUAKERS

George Fox (1624–91) was the founder of the Religious Society of Friends, or Quakers. He wandered around the country, preaching publicly according to his own principles of Christianity, declaring that the established church was corrupt and unnecessary as God was everywhere. He was regularly arrested and imprisoned for sedition and blasphemy. In 1656 he and two friends spent nine miserable weeks in Launceston Gaol, an experience he described in graphic detail:

The place was so noisome that it was observed few that went in did ever come out again in health. There was no house of office in it; and the excrement of the prisoners that from time to time had been put there had not been carried out (as we were told) for many years. So that it was all like mire, and in some places to the tops of the shoes in water and urine; and he would not let us cleanse it, nor suffer us to have beds or straw to lie on. At night some friendly people of the town brought us a candle and a little straw; and we burned a little of our straw to take away the stink. The thieves lay over our heads, and the head jailer in a room by them, over our heads also. It seems the smoke went up into the room where the jailer lay; which put him into such a rage that he took the pots of excrement from the thieves and poured them through a hole upon our heads, till we were so bespattered that we could not touch ourselves nor one another. And the stink increased upon us; so that what with stink, and what with smoke, we were almost choked and smothered. We had the stink under our feet before, but now we had it on our heads and backs also; and he having quenched our straw with the filth he poured down, had made a great smother in the place. Moreover, he railed at us most hideously, calling us hatchet-faced dogs, and such strange names as we had never heard of. In this manner we were obliged to stand all night, for we could not sit down, the place was so full of filthy excrement.

METHODISTS

John (1703–91) and Charles Wesley (1707–88) were the joint founders of Methodism, a branch of Christianity based to a great extent on Bible study and a methodical approach to the scriptures and Christian living. They arrived in Cornwall in 1743 and, after initial resistance from angry mobs, gradually found a ready audience, particularly among the mining communities which responded to the Methodist message of self-improvement and salvation. According to Charles, 'I adored the miracle of grace, which has kept these sheep in the midst of wolves. Well may the despisers behold and wonder. Here is a bush in a fire, burning, yet not consumed! What have they done to crush this rising sect? but lo! they prevail nothing! . . . . Many waters cannot quench this little spark which the Lord hath kindled neither shall the floods of persecution drown it.'

John was likewise encouraged by the way that people were coming round to accept them. After visiting Mevagissey 1757, he wrote that when he had previously been there, 'we had no place in the town. . . . But things are altered now: I preached just over the town, to almost all the inhabitants, and all were as still as night.' By 1780 there were 26 Methodist preaching houses in the county.

Among the Wesleys' followers in Cornwall were a select band of itinerant preachers, notably John Murlin (1722–99), Peter Jaco (1729–81), Richard Rodd (1743–1805), and probably the most well-known of all, Billy Bray (1794–1868), whose father and grandfather had both been pious Methodists, and who was a former drunkard who converted to Methodism and renounced the demon alcohol. Another was William O'Bryan (1778–1868), born William Bryant until changing his name in 1815, founder of the Christian Bible Movement, which had a particularly strong following in the Padstow and Bude areas.

AN EARLY BATTLE

The Battle of Hehil is believed to have been fought in about AD 721, somewhere in Cornwall or possibly Devon. Almost nothing is known about it, beyond its significance as a victory for the West Britons over the Anglo-Saxons and their subsequent securing of the independence of Dumnonia, the Celtic kingdom which later became Cornwall.

THE REBELLION OF 1497

Michael Joseph (Michael An Gof) and Thomas Flamank led a Cornish rebellion against Henry VII's levying of new taxes to finance an invasion of Scotland. Joseph led a march to London in 1497, which began at St Keverne. They joined Flamank and his supporters at Bodmin, but the untrained and poorly armed force of about 8,000 which they led through the south of England, losing several of the less committed along the way, proved no match for the king's superior force which surrounded them and fought a pitched battle at Deptford Bridge on 17 June. At least 300 men were killed, and Flamank was captured, while An Gof fled and was captured at Greenwich. Both were condemned to death a week later in the White Hall at Westminster, hanged, drawn and quartered at Tyburn and their heads displayed on pikestaffs on London Bridge. Just before their execution, An Gof said he would have 'a name perpetual and a fame permanent and immortal', while Thomas Flamank remarked, 'Speak the truth and only then can you be free of your chains'.

Over the centuries 27 June has been celebrated as An Gof Day, with annual events in Bodmin, St Keverne and London dedicated to their memory. On the eastern side of the Norman tower of Redruth Church are two grotesque gargoyles representing Henry VII and his Queen, Elizabeth of York. The headgear on the male figure is very like that in portraits of the king, and it is said that they were created and erected as Cornwall's response to the suppression of the rebellion.

THE COMMON PRAYER DISPUTES

In 1547 the *Book of Common Prayer* in English replaced the old liturgical books in Latin. This move was particularly unpopular in Cornwall, which had long been a bastion of Roman Catholic sympathies. As part of the church's campaign against 'popery', in which traditional religious processions and pilgrimages were made illegal, one of the commissioners appointed by Archbishop Cranmer to remove all symbols of Catholicism from churches in England was William Body. When he came to remove and destroy images from the church at Helston in April 1548 a crowd gathered, seized him, dragged him into the streets and stabbed him to death. Retribution followed swiftly when 28 Cornishmen who were accused of aiding and abetting him were arrested and executed at Launceston Castle. In July 1549 Martin Geoffrey, the parish priest of St Keverne, was taken to London and hanged, after which his head was then cut off and impaled on a spike on London Bridge.

AN ELIZABETHAN MARTYR

In 1576 Cuthbert Mayne, a Roman Catholic priest, became chaplain to Francis Tregian of Golden Manor, Probus. The Bishop of Exeter was ordered to deal severely with Roman Catholics in the west country and on Corpus Christi Day, 8 June 1577, supported by Justices of the Peace and about a hundred armed men, the Sheriff of Cornwall, Richard Grenville, surrounded and raided Tregian's house. He arrested Mayne, wearing the waxen Agnus Dei, strictly prohibited under Elizabethan law, and seized his books and papers. Mayne was paraded through several villages to Launceston Castle, and held in a dungeon for three months.

In September he was tried before Roger Manwood and Sir John Jeffreys on charges including 'traitorously obtaining' a Papal bull, and publishing it at Golden, teaching the ecclesiastical authority of the Pope and denying the queen's ecclesiastical authority while in prison, and celebrating Mass in the papal manner. Found guilty, he was ordered to forfeit all his property and lands and sentenced to life imprisonment. According to the other prisoners, on 27 November Mayne's cell was said to have become full of 'a great light'. He was 'examined' from dawn till dusk after being declared a traitor, and told his life would be spared if he promised to swear on the Bible to renounce his religion and acknowledge the supremacy of Queen Elizabeth as head of the church. He took the Bible in his hands, made the sign of the cross on it, and said, 'The Queen neither ever was, nor is, nor ever shall be the head of the church in England.'

Next day he was dragged through the streets of Launceston and hanged on a gibbet in the marketplace. While still alive, his body was cut down, and he fell with such force that his eye was driven out. His severed head was placed on the castle gate, and quarters of his body were despatched to Bodmin, Tregony, Wadebridge and Barnstaple, where he was born and raised. The first seminary priest to be martyred in England, he was canonised in 1970, and the Catholic Church at Launceston is named after him.

THE ENGLISH CIVIL WAR IN CORNWALL

The Battle of Braddock Down, 19 January 1643, was a brief skirmish culminating in a Royalist victory in which Sir Ralph Hopton defeated the Parliamentary forces under General Ruthin and placed Cornwall once again under Royalist control. About 200 Parliamentary soldiers were killed and 1,500 were taken prisoner.

The Battle of Stratton, 16 March 1643, was another victory under Hopton, this time against the forces of the Earl of Stamford, and confirmed Royalist control of Cornwall. About 300 of the Parliamentary army were left dead on the field, and 1,700 taken prisoner.

The Battle of Lostwithiel was a series of skirmishes in August and early September 1644 in which King Charles's army achieved the last Royalist victory of the war over the Parliamentary forces led by the Earl of Essex, before Cromwell's forces regained the ascendancy. Essex left Sir Philip Skippon, his Sergeant Major General of Foot, in command while he escaped. Skippon surrendered 6,000 infantry, in addition to all his army's guns.

At Pendennis Castle, between March and August 1646, a Royalist garrison comprising about 1,500 men, women and children withstood a siege from the Parliamentary forces for 155 days before surrendering out of starvation.

NEWS OF THE BATTLE OF TRAFALGAR

The people of Cornwall were the first to be told of the British victory at the Battle of Trafalgar on 21 October 1805 and the death of Admiral Lord Nelson. The news was given to local fishermen, who informed the authorities at Penzance. The mayor, Thomas Giddy, made an official announcement at the Assembly Rooms at the Union Hotel. A courier, John Lapenotiere, rode in a post-chaise carriage from Falmouth to London in thirty-eight hours (a journey which normally took one week) to bring the news to king and country.

THE RIOTS IN CAMBORNE

On 7 October 1873 a riot broke out in Camborne after police summoned two miners for trying to rescue a prisoner. Several thousand miners, most armed with sticks and stones, gathered to try and prevent the prisoners from being taken to gaol but were frustrated by the removal of the men to a back way by road instead of rail. The rioters then vented their wrath on the neighbouring buildings; the windows of the magistrates' hall, the Assembly Rooms and the police station were smashed, while the windows of several houses and hotels were also attacked. Every time a policeman was seen, there were groans and derisive cheers, and as another came into the street he was soon forced to seek shelter in the building. Next day two men were arrested, a new contingent of police was summoned from Bodmin, and several special constables were sworn in. Warrants were issued for the arrest of rioters, and when two miners were brought before the Bench, witnesses testified to the police having acted with unnecessary violence. Some residents were leaving the area as they feared further incidents. The magistrates issued an order for all public houses to be closed from 5.00 p.m. till 7.00 a.m. next day, but some of the mob still got into a number of the houses, particularly Newming's Hotel, where they gutted the premises, took the beer and spirits into the street, drank some of them and poured the rest down the gutters. Over the next three days the agitation gradually died down, and several miners were arrested for causing a disturbance.

On 18 April 1892 two Irishmen were sentenced for a brutal assault on another man at Camborne, one of them to two months and the other to six weeks. After the case the prisoners, still accompanied by the police, were followed through the streets by an excited crowd who struck and threw stones at them. An Irishman who had given evidence for the defence was attacked. The mob then went to Cook's Kitchen Mine, about a mile from the town, where they assaulted an Irishman at work. On returning to the town they attacked the Roman Catholic church, smashed the windows, broke open the doors, tore down an image of the Virgin Mary, flung it into the road and trampled it underfoot, while the altar, gas fittings, seats and organ were completely destroyed. The house of Father McKey, the Catholic priest, was attacked and he had to scale a wall to evade his pursuers and a conservatory at the home of Major Pike, a prominent local Roman Catholic, was destroyed. By 10.00 p.m. the town was reported to be completely in the hands of the mob, with the police powerless to act. Next day the magistrates issued an order requiring all public houses in the town to close at 4.00 p.m., and advised residents to remain within their houses during the evening. By midnight the mob was under control. A small crowd assembled and pelted the police, who were ordered to clear the streets. In the rush that ensued, several persons were trampled on and injured. A few roughs went 'on an expedition' to Brea, but returned to Camborne without having done any harm.

PARANOIA IN THE FIRST WORLD WAR

D.H. Lawrence (1885–1930), novelist and poet, and his German wife Frieda came to live at Zennor in December 1915 during the First World War. They stayed at the Tinners Arms, and then rented Higher Tregerthen nearby. While they were there he completed *Women in Love*, which would be published in 1920. Both were very outspoken against the war and the government, and they dreaded the possibility of his being called up for active service because of (and despite) his tubercular condition. Mrs Lawrence made no attempt to conceal her German origins, and the sound of German folk songs could sometimes be heard coming from their house. Their presence in a place near shipping lanes where enemy submarines were inflicting heavy losses on Allied ships was bitterly resented. Lawrence was warned that coastwatchers had long been keeping a close eye on them both, and soon afterwards the police, using their powers under the terms of the Defence of the Realm Act, called on them and ordered them to leave within the week. One chapter of a later novel by Lawrence, *Kangaroo* (1923), was based on the time he spent in the county, while their sojourn in the area forms part of the plot in Helen Dunmore's novel *Zennor in Darkness* (1993).

Father Bernard Walke, curate at St Hilary between 1912 and 1936, was a staunch pacifist and member of a peace society, The Fellowship of Reconciliation. When he attended a meeting in the Labour Hall at Penzance 150 men from the Naval Reserve entered the hall, led by an officer who demanded that he would promise never to speak again on the subject of making peace. When he refused, the men broke up the meeting, some leading the women out of the hall while others smashed furniture and threw pieces out of the windows. Walke tried to leave the hall, but a curtain was thrown over his head, and he was knocked unconscious, only to come round and find himself being guarded by two soldiers who told the troublemakers that they would gladly take on 'the whole bloody navy' if they had to. He walked free, but during the remaining years of the war he was suspected by some of his neighbours of helping to prepare the enemy for a landing on Marazion beach. A man who had regularly given him lifts in his car since he arrived in St Hilary told him angrily that he was nothing but a German spy, in the pay of the Pope and the Kaiser, and deserved to hang from one of his tallest trees. Nevertheless the trouble soon died down. He later wrote his memoirs, *Twenty Years at St Hilary* (1935).

CORNWALL'S ROYAL REGIMENT

The Duke of Cornwall's Light Infantry, created in Cornwall in 1881, saw action during the First World War on the Western Front, notably in France, Flanders, and also as far afield as Salonika, Macedonia and Palestine. During the Second World War, soldiers fought throughout much of north-west Europe, the Rhineland and North Africa. The Infantry Regimental Museum at Bodmin was opened in 1925.

LOCAL RAF STATIONS

St Mawgan, opened as civilian airfield 1933, requisitioned at start of Second World War and named RAF Trebelzu, renamed RAF St Mawgan 1943; RAF remain on a reduced area, though airfield part of camp closed 2008.

Cleave, put under maintenance 1945 and later became a government signals station.

Predannack Airfield, went into care and maintenance 1946, taken over by Royal Navy 1958.

Davidstowmoor, closed 1945.

Perranporth, decommissioned 1946.

St Eval, closed 1959.

VICTORIA CROSS WINNERS

The following VC winners are buried in Cornwall. Only those marked with an asterisk were also Cornish by birth.

Captain Stephen Beattie (1908–75), RN, won at St Nazaire, France 1942, buried Ruan Minor

Major Herbert Carter (1874–1916), 101st Grenadiers, Indian Army, won at Jidballi, Somaliland 1903, buried St Erth

Boatswain Henry Cooper (1825–93), RN, won at Sea of Azov, Crimea 1855, buried Antony

*Sergeant Horace Curtis (1891–1968), 2nd Battalion Royal Dublin Fusiliers, won at Le Cateau, France 1918, buried Truro

Private John Divane (1823–88), 60th Rifles, King's Royal Rifle Corps, won at Delhi (Indian Mutiny) 1857, buried Penzance

Lieutenant-Colonel Harold Ervine-Andrews (1911–95), East Lancashire Regiment, won at Canal de Bergues, France 1940, buried Bodmin

Captain Wilfred St Aubyn Malleson (1896–1975), RN, won at Gallipoli 1915, buried Truro

*Quartermaster William Odgers (1834–73), RN, won at Omata, New Zealand, 1860, buried Saltash

Captain Robert Phillips (1895–1968), 13th Battalion Warwickshire Regiment, won at River Hai, Kut, Mesopotamia, 1917, buried St Veep

Able Seaman William Savage (1912–42), RN, won at St Nazaire, France 1942, buried Falmouth

Boatswain (First Class) *John Sheppard* (1817–84), RN, won at Sebastopol Bay, Crimea 1855, buried Padstow

* *Able Seaman Joseph Trewavas* (1835–1905), RN, won at Sea of Azov, Crimea 1855, buried Paul, near Newlyn

Wing Commander Guy Gibson, VC (1918–44), noted for leading the 'Dam Busters' raid which destroyed two large dams in the Ruhr area during the Second World War, was not buried in Cornwall but lived at Porthleven for part of his childhood

THE CORNISH HERO OF 9/11

Rick Rescorla

Born in Hayle in 1939, Rick joined the army in 1957, then the police force in London, then subsequently enlisted in the American army and became an American citizen, serving with the forces in Vietnam. In 1985 he joined financial services firm Dean Witter as security director, and when it merged with Morgan Stanley, became director of security in the World Trade Center. When the WTC tower was struck on 11 September 2001 he helped most of his fellow employees to safety before the building collapsed, losing his own life in the process. His body was never recovered. In 2003 he was posthumously awarded the White Cross of Cornwall by the Stannary Parliament.

GHOSTS, WITCHES AND LEGENDS

Battling Billy of Polperro

Battling Billy, landlord of the Halfway House Inn, was also a smuggler who used a hearse to bring his contraband in from the beach. On one occasion – in fact, his last – the brandy was being brought off the ship by daylight, but the revenue officers had been looking out for him and this time they caught him red-handed. As he was driving away, they took aim, shot him in the neck and killed him instantly. However his whip-hand continued to drive the horses back along the road to his inn, but as they reached Polperro, the vehicle carried on straight down the main street, off the quayside and into the harbour. His ghost is still said to haunt the narrow cobbled streets.

The Spirits of Pengersick Castle

This is sometimes said to be the most haunted place in Cornwall, if not Britain, though several others would probably make the same claim. Among the ghosts believed to have been seen there are a 13-year-old girl who apparently danced to her death from the battlements, two murdered women who are still seeking justice against their killers, and the spirit of a man who was strangled to death and stabbed is seen by anybody who stands in front of a particular fireplace.

Jack and Cormoran

Jack was the son of a farmer near Land's End during the reign of King Arthur, at a time when everybody was terrified of the giant Cormoran. A reward was offered to the person who would slay him, and being too small to contemplate any thoughts of physical combat, Jack decided to lure him to his doom instead. He persuaded him to leave St Michael's Mount and come into a specially dug pit. Now trapped, Cormoran was easy prey for Jack who administered a fatal blow by striking him in the head with an axe.

The Giant Bolster

The giant Bolster was said to be able to put one foot on the cliffs of St Agnes and the other on Carn Brea, near Camborne, about 7 miles away. He was notorious for his temper, which might have improved had St Agnes reciprocated his affections. As she was keen to repulse him, she decided to try to set him an impossible task, namely filling a hole on the cliffs at Chapel Porth with his own blood. Little did he, unlike her, realise that it was not a hole, but a pit which ran into the sea. His attempts to carry out the task foundered as he died from loss of blood. To this day there is a large red stain, said to be the result of his futile endeavours.

The Wrath of Portreath

Sometimes known as Ralph, he lived in a large cavern often known as his cupboard at Portreath. A merciless creature, he lay in wait for ships passing by, then seized them and either killed everyone on board or took them to eat for his evening meal, meanwhile helping himself to any treasure that might be aboard. When ships tried to stay out of his way by sailing further out to sea, he hurled rocks, which were no more than pebbles to him although they might be huge boulders to anybody of normal stature. At low tide the rocks are still visible.

WITCHCRAFT TRIALS

During the seventeenth century, about a dozen witch trials were held at Launceston. One of the towers at Launceston Tower was known as the Witch's Tower, because of a belief that witches were burnt at its base, though under English law all those convicted of witchcraft were always hanged. In the 1650s a woman was accused by her neighbours of the crime, and she sought revenge by implicating several others, some of whom were put to death. In July 1686 Jane Nicholas was accused of bewitching John Tonken, aged about 15, tormenting him, and appearing before him, sometimes in human form, 'at other times like a Cat; whereupon the boy would shriek, and cry out that he could not see her, laying his hands over his Eyes and Mouth, and would say with a loud voice, she is putting things into my Mouth, she will choke me, she will poison me'. In later visions she appeared in the shape of a mouse, and left through the window, but would never give him her name. She told him he would not be well until he had vomited nutshells, pins and nails. He brought up straws, rushes, pins, brambles, needles and nails, but his tormentor always appeared beforehand to warn him whenever he was going to vomit. She was charged and put on trial but found not guilty.

HAUNTED PUBS

Jamaica Inn, Bolventor

A whole book could be written about the various legends and ghosts said to be associated with this old posting house. One tells of a sailor who was drinking at the bar when he was called outside by a stranger to discuss business. He was never seen alive again, and next morning his body was found dead on the moor. His ghost has returned to the bar on many an occasion to finish that drink. He is thought to be connected with the lonely figure in seaman's clothes, which is said to sit on the low wall outside the inn without talking or even moving.

Crumplehorn Inn, Polperro

A sixteenth-century mill house, it became an inn in 1972. One morning the landlord awoke to see a figure in front of the bedroom mirror, smoking a cigarette, clasping its head and complaining of a severe headache. Thinking it was his wife, he asked her if she was all right – and then realised that she was in bed next to him. When he turned to look at the figure again it had gone. Both of them repeatedly heard the whispering voices of a man and a woman in the loft above their room. The landlady, who possessed psychic powers, was sure the man had been a soldier during the First World War who had deserted and was hiding in the loft with his girlfriend, but was found, captured and sent to the trenches where he was killed. His spirit and that of his girlfriend, she believed, had returned to haunt the premises.

Wellington Hotel, Boscastle

An eighteenth-century coachman, wearing a frock coat, frilled shirt and leather boots and gaiters, is said to walk round the hotel and then suddenly disappear through one of the walls.

The Punch Bowl Inn, Lanreath

During medieval times, the village rector was entertaining his curate to dinner one evening. They ran out of wine, so he got up from the table and went to fetch another bottle from the cellar, but slipped on the top step and fell to his death. It may, however, not have been an accident, but instead the result of a swift push from the curate who was having an affair with his host's wife behind his back. Next day, the rector returned to haunt not only the curate but also everyone in the village as a black cockerel, attacking everyone in its way. When the terrified villagers ran away, it went in search of them and flew through the window of the inn, then into an earthenware oven. The maid slammed the door shut, but there was to be no *Coq noir* on the menu. Instead the landlord employed a mason to cover the oven with cement in order to trap the fearsome bird inside. Its spirit allegedly stalks the premises, seeking vengeance for its untimely fate.

The Star, Truro

An old coaching house in which a young girl was apparently murdered some two or three centuries ago, and whose spirit still returns during the evenings to haunt the premises.

The Dolphin, Penzance

A ghost dressed in a tricorn hat and lace ruffles, who wanders around the rooms, is said to be an Elizabethan sea captain who was murdered by his crew. Alternatively, as the notorious Judge Jeffreys turned the inn's dining room into a temporary court and the cellars into a gaol after the Duke of Monmouth's unsuccessful rebellion against his uncle James II in 1685, he might be one of the more noble Cornish Protestant victims who was captured and executed for treason.

LEGENDARY CREATURES

Bucca

A fairy or hobgoblin thought to be a spirit which lived in tin mines and coastal communities, sometimes granting wishes in exchange for food, or an ancient pagan deity of the sea. The name of bucca or pwca comes from Scandinavia. In the nineteenth century, fishermen used to venerate Bucca with offerings of fish, particularly on beaches around Mousehole and Newlyn. Fishermen and sailors believed that Bucca's voice was carried on the winds, and storms from a south-westerly direction were known as 'Bucca calling'.

The Owlman

Two sightings were reported in 1976 and 1978 of a large dark winged creature similar to an owl but as large as a human figure, with pointed ears and pincer-like claws, in the woods close to Mawnan Church. A similar one, a brown-grey creature about 5ft tall with large black feet and huge toes, was reported at the same site in 1989. Despite the reports of two paranormal researchers, it is thought to be a hoax, and more likely an eagle owl, one of the largest European owls with a wingspan of up to 6ft, not a native species in Britain but sometimes kept in captivity by falconry enthusiasts.

Pixies

Small fairy-like creatures said to be found in the high moorland areas of Cornwall and Dartmoor, with pointed ears and eyes pointed upwards towards the temples, wearing green clothes and pointed hats, are believed to inhabit stone circles and standing stones. The name pixie is thought to come from the Swedish 'pyske', or little fairy, though it is claimed that piskie is Celtic in origin. During the early Christian era they were thought to be the souls of small children who had died without being baptised. In the nineteenth century it was believed that they were descended from the tribes of ancient Britain who painted their skins blue with woad.

One legend tells that at Trevose Head about 600 pixies gathered dancing and laughing in a circle that had appeared upon the turf until one, Omfra, lost his laugh. He searched among the barrows of the ancient kings of Cornwall on St Breock Downs and waded through Dozmary Pool on Bodmin Moor, after which his laugh was restored to him by King Arthur, who had turned into a chough.

The Queen of the Pixies, or Piskeys, Joan the Wad, is often portrayed on charms carried or worn to bring good luck.

Spriggans

Grotesquely ugly creatures said to be found in the West Penwith area at old ruins and barrows, acting as fairy bodyguards guarding buried treasure. Though small, they are said to be able to swell to a much larger, even giant, size. They are thought to be capable of thieving, aggravating those who have offended them, stealing children and leaving ugly changelings in their place, and sending storms to destroy crops at harvest time.

The Merry Maidens stone circle of St Buryan

Nineteen maidens at St Buryan repeatedly danced on the Sabbath, and were warned that if they persisted in doing so, they would be turned into stone as a punishment. Disregarding the warning, they paid the penalty, and the pipers who had been playing for them were sentenced to share the same fate, becoming two megaliths north-east of the circle. A variation on the story suggests that the pipers heard the church clock in St Buryan striking midnight, realised they were breaking the sabbath, and started to run up the hill away from the maidens who continued to dance without accompaniment. Similar tales are told to explain the origins of stone circles at Tregeseal and Boskednan.

Doom Bar

A mermaid at Padstow was said to guide ships up the estuary, or alternatively pretend to do so, but would actually be spying on them as they sailed into harbour. One day she was sitting on a rock at Hawkers Cove when she met a man, and they fell deeply in love. Either she tried to lure him beneath the waves with her and he refused, or he asked her to marry him but she turned him down. He lost his temper and shot her dead. Another version says that a fisherman shot her because he thought she was a seal preying on the catch which provided him with a living. With her dying breath she pronounced a curse on Padstow, the town and the harbour together, rendering it unsafe. A storm then blew up, wrecking several boats and creating a great treacherous bank of sand known as the Doom Bar.

The Mermaid of Zennor

Every evening a young chorister, named Matthew Trewhella, sang the final hymn at Zennor Church as a solo. A mermaid who lived nearby in Pendour Cove and was particularly fond of music visited the church, wearing a long dress to conceal her tail. At first she used to stay just long enough to watch him sing, but later she stayed around longer, as she was keen to know him a little better. Eventually they became rather attached to each other, but she knew that nothing could become of it, because she had to return to the sea. When she prepared to take her leave, he begged her not to go, and asked her where she had come from. When she told him, he vowed that in future he would always follow her wherever she went. As good as his word, he carried her back to the cove and followed her beneath the waves. Nobody ever saw him again. To this day, it is said that those who sit above Pendour Cove on fine summer evenings can still hear him singing on the breeze.

Dozmary Pool

According to Arthurian legend, this is where King Arthur rowed out to the Lady of the Lake and received the sword Excalibur, and also where Sir Bedivere returned Excalibur as Arthur lay dying after the Battle of Camlann.

Another tale associated with the pool is that of Jan Tregeagle, a notorious seventeenth-century magistrate who was rumoured to have murdered his wife, and made a pact with the devil in return for money and power. At his death, he was condemned to lie at the bottom, and his ghost is still said to howl across Bodmin Moor.

CORNWALL'S LOST KINGDOM

Although the date has often been disputed, on or around 11 November 1099 a great storm blew up over the lost land of Lyonesse, a small country beyond Land's End, which comprised several fine cities and about 140 churches. Within a few hours the sea swept across it, submerging it beneath the waves, and everybody was drowned except for one man, who rode a white horse up to high ground at Perranuthnoe before the waves could overwhelm him as well. The Trevelyan family took the design for its coat of arms, showing a white horse rising from the waves, from this story. All that remained of the land were mountain peaks to the west, which some believe to be the Isles of Scilly. Others maintain that it is 8 miles north-east of the Scillies and 18 miles west of Land's End, while others say that it is a sunken forest in Mount's Bay, and its petrified tree stumps are visible at low tide. Some Christians regarded it as Cornwall's own Sodom and Gomorrah, a land of debauchery and sinful living which had provoked divine wrath and ultimately its destruction. Over the years people have claimed to have heard the church bells of Lyonesse ringing beneath the waves, or seen the towers, domes, spires and battlements beneath the waves while standing on the cliffs at Land's End, while fishermen have also been said to find small parts of the buildings in their fishing nets.

LOCAL CUSTOMS AND FESTIVALS

Golowan Festival

Held in Penzance, this began probably in the mid-eighteenth century, part of a much wider tradition of midsummer festivals where bonfires were lit on hilltops on Midsummer's Eve, and fell into abeyance in the Victorian era but was revived in 1991. Spanning three days in late June, it features performances from local musicians, exhibitions by artists, street fairs and processions.

Lowender Peran

An annual five-day festival held at Perranporth in late October. Celebrating the heritage of Cornwall's traditional music, dance, songs, storytelling and the county's links with Ireland, Brittany, the Isle of Man and Scotland, and held in honour of St Piran, it includes concerts, ceilidhs, and music and dance workshops.

Helston Flora Day

Held annually, on 8 May or thereabouts if it falls on a Sunday or Monday, this is another celebration with pagan origins to mark the passing of winter and the coming of spring. Four dances are staged, the first at 7.00 a.m. with ladies in summer frocks, gentlemen in white shirts, dark grey trousers and ties bearing the town crest; the second at 9.50 a.m. with schoolchildren dressed in white; the third at midday with the 'county gentry', ladies in ball gowns and hats, gentlemen in morning dress; and the last at 5.00 p.m. for the town tradespeople. Music is provided by folk bands on fiddles, bagpipes, brass and wind instruments, and shops are decorated with spring flowers.

Padstow Obby Oss Festival

Held annually on 1 May, this probably has its origins in an ancient fertility rite, probably the old Celtic festival of Beltane. It begins at midnight on May Eve, with people from the town gathering outside the Golden Lion to sing the 'Night Song', led by the Obby Oss Choir. By the morning, the town has been decorated with greenery and spring flowers such as bluebells and cowslips, and flowers placed around the maypole. Male dancers lead a procession through the streets dressed as one of the two Obby Osses, wearing masks and black frame-hung capes as they try to catch young maidens passing through the town. Two parades follow, the 'Mayer' in top hat, followed by a band with accordions and drums, then the Oss and the Teaser. Celebrations continue until the evening, with the Osses meeting at the maypole.

Padstow Mummers or Darkie Day

On Boxing Day and New Year's Day at Padstow, residents make themselves up with black faces and parade through the town singing minstrel songs. This had its roots in old British midwinter celebrations, and is also thought to celebrate slave ships docking at the town, although no records have been found to substantiate the latter. In recent years 'Darkie Day' has been criticised on the grounds of being racist, and efforts to persuade the police to press charges have not been successful, although it has been modified and renamed 'Mummers' Day' in order not to cause offence.

Trevithick Day

Held on the last Saturday of April, this is a celebration in Camborne of the life and achievements of Richard Trevithick. It includes model exhibitions, street entertainment, a fun fair, the Bal Maidens and Miners Dance led by Camborne Town Band, a parade of miniature engines, display of steam engines and finally the steam parade.

John Knill celebrations, St Ives

Held at St Ives once every five years on 25 July, the Feast Day of St James the Apostle, the first was in 1801 and the most recent in 2011. They are staged in memory of John Knill (1733–1811), mayor of the town in 1767 and collector of customs for over twenty years. It is led by ten girls (the daughters of fishermen, seamen or tinners), two widows, fiddlers, and three trustees – the mayor, the customs officer and vicar, accompanied by the mace bearer and master of ceremonies. They lead a procession from the Guildhall to the Knill Steeple, a three-sided obelisk of local granite, 50ft high, on a hill 1 mile from the town centre, which Knill built in 1782 intending it to be his mausoleum although it was never used. As they go on their way, they sing the 100th Psalm, 'All people that on earth do dwell'. They dance around the steeple three times and the vicar says the blessing, then they return to the town centre where refreshments are provided.

Nickanan Night

Sometimes known as Peasen Monday, Hall Monday or, in West Cornwall, Roguery Night, this is an annual occasion on the eve of Shrove Tuesday when young people play practical jokes, or knock on doors and run away, not unlike 'trick or treat'. According to journalist Thomas Quiller-Couch, writing in the mid-nineteenth century:

> . . . about the dusk of the evening, it is the custom for boys, and, in some cases, for those who are above the age of boys, to prowl about the streets with short clubs, and to knock loudly at every door, running off to escape detection on the slightest sign of a motion within. If, however, no attention is excited, and especially if any article should be discovered negligently exposed, or carelessly guarded, then the things are carried away; and on the following day are discovered displayed in some conspicuous place, to expose the disgraceful want of vigilance supposed to characterise the owner. The time when this is practised is called 'Nicka-nan night' and the individuals concerned are supposed to represent some imps of darkness, that seize on and expose unguarded moments.

In Polperro and other villages, people would make a straw figure, called 'Jack o'Lent', parade it around the streets where things would be thrown at it, and then burn it on a bonfire, as in Guy Fawkes Night.

Midsummer customs and superstitions

It is said in Cornwall that if a young unmarried woman stands at midnight on Midsummer's Eve in the porch of the parish church, she will see passing in front of her in procession everyone who will die in the parish during the coming year. Needless to say, few have been brave enough to dare try the experiment. Stories have been told of those who have, and have seen shadows of themselves. From that day onwards they have pined, and before midsummer comes around again they have been laid to rest in the village graveyard.

Less forbidding county superstitions relating to midsummer day say that if a young woman takes off the shift which she has been wearing, washes it, turns it inside out, and hangs it across the back of a chair, then waits until midnight, the man she will marry appears and turns the garment over. Another says that if a young lady walks backwards into the garden on the same day and picks a rose, she will find out who is to become her husband. The rose has to be sewn up in a paper bag, and put aside in a dark drawer until Christmas Day. On Christmas morning it must be opened in silence, and the rose must be pinned to the garment on her breast, so she can wear it to church. A young man will either ask her if he can take the rose, or else take it without asking, and he is the man she will marry.

It was also said that all Cornish witches regarded Trews, near Zennor, as their home. On midsummer eve they would light fires on the nearby granite dolmens, or prehistoric chamber tombs, in the hills, then assemble there to renew their vows with the Prince of Darkness. The precise spot where they gathered was marked by a large pile of granite blocks, called the Witches' Rock. To touch it was thought to be a safeguard against bad luck, though it has since been removed.

Cattle and oxen at Christmas

It is said that all the oxen and cows at a farm in the parish of St Germans, and also in parts of west Devon, can be found on their knees when the clock strikes midnight on Christmas Eve. In the late eighteenth century a man living on the edge of St Stephen's Down, near Launceston, wanted to test this belief. Shortly before midnight he and several others stood watching the beasts in their stalls, and observed the two eldest oxen fall upon their knees at the exact time, as they made 'a cruel moan, like Christian creatures'.

Safety in Redruth

Although it is hardly a major consideration for parents who wish to safeguard any of their malevolent children from the ultimate sentence in this day and age, it was often said that no child who was baptised with the water from St Ruth's Well near Portreath would ever be hanged.

THE COUNTY COAT OF ARMS

Cornwall's coat of arms was granted in April 1939. It shows a fisherman, to represent the maritime connections, and a tin miner, representing mineral wealth and industrial heritage. Between them is a chough, resting one claw on a ducal coronet. They are jointly supporting a shield, enclosed by waves, displaying fifteen gold bezants arranged in an inverted triangle, said to be the ransom which the Cornish had to pay to ensure the release of the king's eldest son who had been captured by Saracens during the Crusades. Underneath is the motto, 'One And All', to indicate that they had all helped together to raise the sum. There is some doubt as to this legend as England's main crusading king, Richard I, is believed to have never had any children.

When Cornwall acquired administrative status in 2009, with a new body replacing the county and district councils, the coat of arms was replaced by a rather uninspiring computer-generated logo of patterned lines in black, gold and yellow. Thankfully the new council soon bowed to public indignation and restored the time-honoured coat of arms.

THE COUNTY FLAG

Cornwall's flag is that of St Piran. It shows a white cross which represents molten tin oozing out of a black rock which Piran used when building his fireplace. As the flames became hotter, the tin smelted out of the rock. It is flown not only throughout the county on St Piran's Day, 5 March, but also on Trevithick Day at Camborne in April, the Obby Oss Festival, Padstow and Helston's Flora Day, both in May, as well as at the Gorseth Kernow, and at Cornish rugby matches.

9

SPORTING CORNWALL

SPORTING PERSONALITIES

Bob Fitzsimmons (1863–1917), born at Helston, emigrated to the United States as a young man and became the first boxer to win three world titles, middleweight in 1891, heavyweight in 1897, and light-heavyweight in 1903. After retiring from sport he became an evangelist.

Jack (John Frederick) *Crapp* (1912–81), born at St Columb Major, was the first Cornishman to play cricket for England, making his first Test appearance against Australia at Old Trafford in 1948. Until 1984 he was the only Cornishman to wear an England cap.

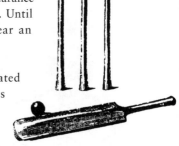

John Kendall-Carpenter (1926–90), educated at Truro, rugby footballer who started as a club player for Penzance and Newlyn, subsequently became President of the Rugby Football Union, and Captain of the England Rugby team.

Richard Sharp (1938–) began his sporting career playing rugby for Redruth, and later played for England while studying at Oxford. Bernard Cornwell's character Richard Sharpe is said to be based on him.

Jonah Barrington (1941–), born at Morwenstow, squash player who won the British Open title six times between 1967 and 1973.

Sebastian Coe (1956–), athlete who won four Olympic medals as a middle-distance runner in 1980 and 1984. After retiring from sport he served as Conservative MP for Falmouth and Camborne from 1992 to 1997, and later became Chairman of the London Organising Committee for the 2012 Olympic Games.

Nigel Martyn (1966–), born at St Austell, footballer who played for Crystal Palace, thus becoming in 1989 the first goalkeeper to attract a million-pound transfer fee in English football, then moved on to Leeds United and Everton.

Phil Vickery (1976–), rugby footballer who initially played with Bude and Redruth clubs, then joined the England squad, was appointed captain of the England squad touring Argentina in 2002, and played in all seven matches of the winning 2003 Rugby World Cup tournament.

COUNTY FOOTBALL TEAMS

The name is followed by the date founded and their home ground.

Bodmin Town FC	1889	Priory Park
Falmouth Town AFC	1949	Bickland Park
Helston Athletic FC	1896	Kellaway Park
Launceston FC	1891	Pennygillam
Liskeard Athletic FC	1946	Lux Park
Millbrook AFC	1896	Mill Park
Mullion FC	date unknown	Clifden Parc
Newquay AFC	1890	Mount Wise
Penryn Athletic FC	1963	Kernick Road
Penzance AFC	1888	Penlee Park
Porthleven FC	1896	Gala Parc
St Austell FC	1890	Poltair Park
St Blazey AFC	1896	Blaise Park
Saltash United FC	1946	Kimberley Stadium
Torpoint Athletic FC	1887	The Mill
Truro City FC	1889	Treyew Road
Wadebridge Town FC	1894	Bodieve Park

RUGBY FOOTBALL TEAMS

The Cornwall Rugby Football Union (CRFU) was founded in 1883 and includes the following teams, with date founded and their home ground where known.

Bodmin, *c.* 1886, disbanded *c.* 1912, refounded 1969, Clifden Park
Bude RFC, 1966, Bencoolen Meadow
Callington RFC, 1996, Duchy College, Stoke Climsland
Camborne RFC, 1878, Crane Park
Cornish Pirates, founded as Penzance & Newlyn RFC in 1945 after merging
  of Penzance RFC and Newlyn RFC, Mennaye Field, Penzance
Falmouth RFC, Recreation Ground
Hayle RFC, Marsh Lane
Helston RFC, 1965, King George V Playing Field

Illogan Park RFC, Paynters Lane End
Lankelly-Fowey RFC, 1968, Lankelly Farm
Launceston RFC, Polson Bridge
Liskeard Leopards Womens RFC,
    Liskeard School and Community
    Centre
Liskeard-Looe RFC, Lux Park
Newquay Hornets RFC, 1933, Newquay
    Sports Centre, Tretherras Road
Penryn RFC, 1872, Kernick Road
Perranporth RFC, Ponsmere Valley
Redruth Albany RFC, 1929, Trewirgie
Redruth RFC, 1875, Recreation Ground
Saltash RFC, Moorlands Lane
St Agnes RFC, Enys Park
St Austell RFC, Tregorrick Park
St Day RFC, Telegraph Hill
St Ives RFC, Alexandra Road
St Just RFC, Tregeseal, Nancherrow
Stithians RFC, Church Road
Truro RFC, St Clements Hill
Wadebridge Camels RFC, Molesworth Field

CRICKET CLUBS

The following are some of the top cricket clubs in the county, with their
home ground or headquarters.

Bude CC, Crooklets Cricket Ground
Callington CC, New Road
Camborne CC, North Roskear Road
Falmouth CC, Trescobeas Road
Gorran CC, The Cricket Field
Grampound Road CC, Grampound Road, Truro
Hayle CC, Tresdale Parc, Connor Downs
Launceston CC, Cricket Ground, Lawhitton
Luckett CC, Chapel Field

Newquay CC, Sports Centre, Whitegate Road
Paul CC, Trungle Moor, Penzance
Penzance CC, St Clare
Redruth CC, Trewirgie
St Austell CC, Bethel
St Just CC, Cape Cornwall Road
Troon CC, Treslothan Road
Truro CC, Boscawen Park
Wadebridge CC, Egloshayle Road
Werrington CC, Werrington Park,
    Launceston

SURFING

Surfing is said to have been introduced into Britain by soldiers returning from the war in South Africa early in the nineteenth century, copying Hawaiian boards. By the 1920s Cornwall was being recognised as the surfing centre of the UK.

In 1994 the World Lifesaving Championships were held for the first time in Britain at Fistral Beach, Newquay, with over 1,500 competitors worldwide from countries including most European states and also the USA, Canada, Australia and Japan. In addition to competitive events there are also annual charity fixtures, such as that which takes place annually at Chapel Porth Beach near St Agnes where surfers of all ages use traditional wooden belly boards, with funds raised going to the National Trust and the RNLI.

SURFING SCHOOLS

Gwithian Academy of Surfing
Shore Surf School, Hayle
Surf's Up! Surf School, Polzeath
BSA National Surfing Centre, Fistral Beach, Newquay
English Surf Federation Surf School, Newquay

Escape Surf School, Newquay
Reef Surf School, Newquay
Sennen Surf School
Cornwall Surf Academy, Newquay & St Ives
Big Blue Surf School, Bude
Outdoor Adventure, Widemouth Bay
121 Surf Coach, Watergate Bay

PILOT GIG CLUBS

Bude PGC
Cadgwith GC
Cape Cornwall GC
Caradon PGC
Cornish Pilot Gig Association
Coverack GC
RNAS Culdrose GC
Devoran GC
East Caradon (Saltash) GC
Falmouth GC
Fowey GC
Hayle GC
Helford GC
Looe GC

Mevagissey GC
Mount's Bay GC
Newquay GC
Padstow GC
Porthleven GC
Par Bay GC
Port Isaac GC
St Goran GC
Rame GC
Rock Rowing Club
Roseland GC
St Ives GC
Truro GC
Zennor GC, Penzance

SAILING CLUBS

East Looe Sailing Club
Falmouth School of Sailing
Falmouth, Royal Cornwall Yacht Club
Flushing Sailing Club
Fowey Sailing School
Fowey, Royal Fowey Yacht Club
Helford River Sailing Club
Marazion, Mount's Bay Sailing Club
Mevagissey Sailing School

Mylor Yacht Harbour
Mylor, Restronguet Sailing Club
Penzance Sailing Club
Rock Sailing Club
Roseland Paddle and Sail
St Mawes Sailing Club

MOTOR RACING

Davidstow Circuit, at RAF Davidstow Moor, opened in 1952 and held three Formula One meetings. The circuit was only 2.6 miles in length and its closure in 1955 was attributed to poor weather conditions which made it unsuitable for hosting such events on a long-term basis.

OLYMPIC FLAME

On 18 May 2012 the Olympic flame from Athens arrived on board a British Airways airbus at RNAS Culdrose, carried in a lantern by the Princess Royal and lit on British soil by former England football captain David Beckham. Owing to what the county council later called 'a confusion of maps', the route taken through Cornwall was not precisely as advertised in advance, resulting in a question on the satirical news quiz TV programme *Have I Got News For You?* later that week, 'What caused confusion in Cornwall?' One panellist, comedian Andy Hamilton, said, 'Well, they're Cornish, aren't they? They'll always be confused in Truro.' Dan Rogerson, MP for Cornwall North, claimed that the gag proved the Cornish were discriminated against as a group and made a formal complaint to the BBC and the Equalities and Human Rights Commission, saying such comments would not be tolerated if aimed at the Scottish, Welsh or any other nationality or cultural minority.

10

A CORNISH MISCELLANY

CORNWALL ACCORDING TO DANIEL DEFOE

Daniel Defoe (*c.* 1660–1731) was one of the first writers to describe travelling through his native land, in *A tour through the whole island of Great Britain* (1724–6), although there is some doubt as to whether he actually visited all the places he described, or relied partly on information from friends who had done so. However, he had plenty to say about various Cornish towns.

He called Saltash:

> . . . a little, poor, shattered town . . . (it) seems to be the ruins of a larger place; and we saw many houses, as it were, falling down, and I doubt not but the mice and rats have abandoned many more, as they say they will when they are likely to fall. . . . This town has a kind of jurisdiction upon the River Tamar down to the mouth of the port, so that they claim anchorage of all small ships that enter the river; their coroner sits upon all dead bodies that are found drowned in the river and the like, but they make not much profit of them. There is a good market here, and that is the best thing to be said of the town . . .

Liskeard was

> . . . a considerable town, well built; has people of fashion in it . . . [it] was once eminent, had a good castle, and a large house . . . also remarkable for a very great trade in all manufactures of leather, such as boots, shoes, gloves, purses, breaches, etc.; and some spinning of late years is set up here, encouraged by the woollen manufacturers of Devonshire.

St Germans was

> . . . now a village, decayed, and without any market, but the largest parish in the whole county – in the bounds of which is contained seventeen villages. . . . In the neighbourhood of these towns are many pleasant seats of the Cornish gentry, who are indeed very numerous, though their estates may not be so large as is usual in England; yet neither are they despicable in that part; and in particular this may be said of them – that as they generally live cheap, and are more at home than in other counties, so they live more like gentlemen, and keep more within bounds of their estates than the English generally do, take them all together. Add to this that they are the most sociable, generous, and to one another the kindest, neighbours that are to be found; and as they generally live, as we may say, together (for they are almost always at one another's houses), so they generally intermarry among themselves, the gentlemen seldom going out of the county for a wife, or the ladies for a husband; from whence they say that proverb upon them was raised, viz., That all the Cornish gentlemen are cousins.

He was impressed with the River Fowey:

> . . . very broad and deep here, was formerly navigable by ships of good burthen as high as Lostwithiel – an ancient and once a flourishing but now a decayed town; and as to trade and navigation, quite destitute; which is occasioned by the river being filled up with sands, which, some say, the tides drive up in stormy weather from the sea; others say it is by sands washed from the lead-mines in the hills; the last of which, by the way, I take to be a mistake, the sand from the hills being not of quantity sufficient to fill up the channel of a navigable river, and, if it had, might easily have been stopped by the townspeople from falling into the river. . . . This town retains, however, several advantages which support its figure – as, first, that it is one of the Coinage Towns, as I call them; or Stannary Towns, as others call them; the common gaol for the whole Stannary is here, as are also the County Courts for the whole county of Cornwall.

'Passing from hence,' he recorded:

> . . . and ferrying over Foy River or the River Foweth (call it as you
> please), we come into a large country without many towns in it of note,
> but very well furnished with gentlemen's seats, and a little higher up with
> tin-works. The sea making several deep bays here, they who travel by
> land are obliged to go higher into the country to pass above the water,
> especially at Trewardreth Bay, which lies very broad, above ten miles
> within the country . . .

Next, he found:

> . . . six or seven very considerable places upon this haven and the
> rivers from it – viz., Grampound, Tregony, Truro, Penryn, Falmouth,
> St. Maws, and Pendennis. . . . The town of Falmouth, as big as all
> the three, and richer than ten of them, sends none; which imports no
> more than this – that Falmouth itself is not of so great antiquity as
> to its rising as those other towns are; and yet the whole haven takes
> its name from Falmouth, too, unless, as some think, the town took
> its name from the haven, which, however, they give no authority to
> suggest.

After writing briefly about the fortifications at St Mawes and Pendennis he
dwelt on Falmouth, which was in his view:

> . . . by much the richest and best trading town in this county, though not
> so ancient as its neighbour town of Truro; and indeed is in some things
> obliged to acknowledge the seigniority – namely, that in the corporation
> of Truro the person whom they choose to be their Mayor of Truro
> is also Mayor of Falmouth of course. . . . Falmouth is well built, has
> abundance of shipping belonging to it, is full of rich merchants, and has
> a flourishing and increasing trade.

As for Truro, it was:

> . . . a very considerable town, too. . . . This is the particular town
> where the Lord-Warden of the Stannaries always holds his famous
> Parliament of miners, and for stamping of tin. The town is well
> built, but shows that it has been much fuller, both of houses and
> inhabitants, than it is now; nor will it probably ever rise while the

town of Falmouth stands where it does, and while the trade is settled in it as it is.

Penryn he considered to be:

> . . . a very pleasant, agreeable town, and for that reason has many merchants in it, who would perhaps otherwise live at Falmouth. The chief commerce of these towns, as to their sea-affairs, is the pilchards and Newfoundland fishing, which is very profitable to them all. It had formerly a conventual church, with a chantry and a religious house; but they are all demolished, and scarce the ruins of them distinguishable enough to know one part from another.

Helston, he noted:

> . . . admits the sea so into its bosom as to make a tolerable good harbour for ships a little below the town. It is the fifth town allowed for the coining tin, and several of the ships called tin-ships are laden here. This town is large and populous, and has four spacious streets, a handsome church, and a good trade.

Finally he reached Penzance:

> the farthest town of any note west a place of good business, well built and populous, has a good trade, and a great many ships belonging to it, notwithstanding it is so remote. Here are also a great many good families of gentlemen, though in this utmost angle of the nation; and, which is yet more strange, the veins of lead, tin, and copper ore are said to be seen even to the utmost extent of land at low-water mark, and in the very sea – so rich, so valuable, a treasure is contained in these parts of Great Britain, though they are supposed to be so poor, because so very remote from London, which is the centre of our wealth.
>
> Near Penzance, but open to the sea, is that gulf they call Mount's Bay . . . which they call St. Michael's Mount: the seamen call it only the Cornish Mount. It has been fortified, though the situation of it makes it so difficult of access that . . . there needs no fortification; it was once made a prison for prisoners of State, but now it is wholly neglected. There is a very good road here for shipping, which makes the town of Penzance be a place of good resort.

CORNISH ECCENTRICS

Cornwall has had its fair share of eccentric men of the cloth. One was the Revd Thomas Wills, rector of Wendron and Helston, who took up his living in 1784. An ardent sportsman who loved to watch wrestling, and hunted with hounds, he also kept a cow of which he was very fond. When it died he wanted to give the flesh to his hounds, but was dissuaded on the grounds that it might 'infect the kennels through'. He then did the next most charitable thing possible – or maybe not – by sending a messenger around the parish to announce that beef would be distributed freely to the poor. Perhaps he considered the needy were more resistant to infection than his pack. After he died, it was said that his ghost haunted a windowless room at Trenethick House in the parish, until a group of parsons got together and exorcised it at dead of night. When his sister died, she left a request in her will that a portrait of him as a young man in Court suit was to be removed from its frame, rolled up and buried with her in the family vault at Helston.

The Revd Charles Lethbridge, appointed rector of Stoke Climsland in 1805, was well known for his powers of exorcism. One of his parishioners feared that she and her house were haunted by the spirit of her mother, and she would ask him at any hour, day or night, to come and exorcise it, but it was always gone by the time he arrived. At length, his patience wearing a little thin, he asked her how good a daughter she had been. She admitted that once her mother had irritated her so much that she seized her by the hair and pulled her down the stairs, bumping her head on each one until they reached the bottom. He then suggested that her mother's ghost had good reason to behave as it did, and inferring that she got no more than her just desserts, declared that he could not help her. She apologised profusely and repented for her unreasonable behaviour, and the spirit stopped haunting her soon afterwards.

A vicar in a parish on the banks of the Fal, whose name has not come down to posterity, had a habit of sleeping by day and visiting his parishioners by night. After doing his rounds he would go to play the church organ after midnight, with his unmarried sister who kept house for him fast asleep in the pews – whether from sheer exhaustion after working throughout the day or from a lack of appreciation for his musical talents is open to doubt.

The Revd Robert Stephen Hawker (1803–63), Vicar of Morwenstow, used to talk to the birds and gave each of them names. He invited his nine cats into the church, excommunicated one of them for killing a mouse on Sunday, and kept two deer, named Robin Hood and Maid Marian. Once a visiting clergyman came to call, was pinned to the ground by Robin's antlers, and Hawker had to come and rescue him. Always an unusual dresser, he generally wore a blue knitted fisherman's jersey, and over it a three-quarter-length claret or purple coat. If it was very cold, he would add a yellow poncho and scarlet gauntlets. On his feet, reaching up to his knees, were black or brown sea boots, and socks made from wool provided by his own ewe, spun specially by girls from a school at Liskeard. In his hand he carried a walking-stick shaped like a sword, with a cross at the top. To a fellow clergyman who remarked on his striking attire, he answered that at least he did not look like a waiter or an unemployed undertaker. Hawker's Hut, which he built from driftwood on cliffs overlooking the Atlantic Ocean, and where he spent many hours writing poetry, is at present the smallest property owned by the National Trust.

Henry Lawry, a hatter, was renowned for his forthright opinions. One evening in October 1897 he was outside the municipal buildings at Truro where the bishop, the Right Revd John Gott, was giving a reception in conjunction with the Diocesan Conference. Lawry was reported to be shouting offensive remarks about the bishop into carriages bringing the guests, and several times he was asked to leave but at length had to be removed. On appearing in court a few days later he admitted to being disorderly but denied that he was drunk. Mr Flynn, who tried unsuccessfully to take Lawry home, admitted he seemed 'rather excited'. The worst thing he heard him say was, 'Mr Bishop, you haven't called the poor, the lame and the blind; you have got nobody here but the rich. You ought to have called together the poor who have no bread in their cupboards.' Lawry pleaded that he was 'subject to a considerable degree of excitement and natural exuberance and was consequently unable to take things as coolly as others did.' He had not gone there intending to create a disturbance, but when he saw people leaving the conference, he took the opportunity of saying a few things. He felt sad that the bishop had said 'woman was not capable of the same degree of worship as man', as it was woman who 'stuck to the Saviour until the last, when others fled'. To laughter, he said the bishop was a round man in a square hole. When the magistrates retired, Lawry went on addressing those left the court, saying, 'We may as well pass away the time comfortably, you know.' On returning the mayor said the case was one of the most painful which had come before them, considering the defendant's position in town, and as the magistrates were more or less his friends. He imposed a fine of 2*s* 6*d* and costs.

The Revd Frederick Densham, rector at Warleggan from 1931 to 1953, aroused the wrath of his parishioners when he threatened to sell an organ which had been given as a memorial to men killed in the First World War, refused to hold services at convenient times for them, and put barbed wire round the rectory grounds. Local church councillors petitioned the Bishop of Truro to request his removal, but when the Bishop said he saw no reason to do so they resigned en masse and never went near the church again during his incumbency. When attendance slumped to zero, at first he locked it up and went to the better-attended Methodist Chapel nearby, where he would exhort everyone to abstain from such sinful practices as drinking, reading novels, going to the cinema and playing cards. After growing weary of an empty church, and making entries in the service book such as 'No fog, no wind, no rain – no congregation', he allegedly cut out figures from wood and cardboard, placed them in the pews, named them after previous rectors, preached to them, and offered them the sacraments and full absolution. Now a total recluse, he kept savage Alsatian dogs in the grounds of his rectory, dug a moat and declared he wished to be buried there. After his death, when the rectory was examined, it was found that every window had five different catches.

Eric Putnam (died 1984), editor of the *Cornish Times*, ran very successful eye-catching advertising campaigns for his newspaper based on slogans on the back of local buses, such as 'Read by Kilroy', and 'Peter Pan never bathed'. He also attracted considerable publicity when he undertook to insure every reader with a firm of Lloyds underwriters for £20,000 'in the event of him or her being killed or injured by falling debris from the skylab after its re-entry into the earth's atmosphere'. Although a native of Devon, he realised that it was important to establish his local credentials, and so he invented an uncle who had important Cornish connections 'a long time ago'. A practising Catholic, he always began the day with a twenty-minute yoga session, then five minutes of prayers, using all the Cornish saints in succession. He enjoyed champagne and smoked salmon, wore hand-tailored suits and Gucci shoes, and drove an Alfa Romeo, yet unashamedly went to receptions where there was free food and drink provided, would never pay to get into a function if his press pass would grant him instant access, and at café tables would always take some of the packets of milk and sugar provided to use at home. When asked if he considered himself an eccentric he denied it, explaining that he merely had fun with his money.

WHO'S AN APRIL FOOL?

In Cornwall, an April Fool is known as a 'gowk', as in Scotland, or a 'guckaw'.

On 1 April 2012 the people of Porthleven learnt that the foundations of the town's tower had been undermined by winter storms and freezing weather. Originally the Bickford-Smith Institute, built in 1882 and standing 70ft high, a scientific and literary institute including a lending and reference library and subsequently the offices of the town council and clerk, it was the scene of considerable panic when it suddenly shifted one afternoon. Nevertheless, it provided opportunities for the local tourist council, with the distinction of having Britain's only leaning tower. An influx of sightseers and reporters was anticipated, and a councillor contacted Signore Pescedaprile from the Traditional Inclining Tower Society in Pisa, Italy. It was suggested that a Porthleven branch would be founded, and the Pisa branch would be known as the Big Traditional Inclining Tower Society with the Porthleven branch the Small one. Linguists were aware that *Pesce d'aprile* was the Italian for April Fool.

That same morning, motorists crossing the Hayle Causeway were startled to see five penguins standing in the mud. One of them contacted Paradise Park, but was assured that none of its birds were missing. The mystery became clearer when none of them moved, despite the rising tide. They had been carved from wood by Nick Simpson, a St Ives solicitor who put them there before dawn exactly twelve months earlier as well. On each occasion he brought them indoors after dusk, as 'it was getting a bit chilly for them.'

THE CORNISH AND THE *TITANIC*

When RMS *Titanic* crossed the Atlantic in April 1912 on her ill-fated maiden voyage, of the 2,223 people on board were forty passengers whose home addresses were in Cornwall. Nine were travelling second-class and the rest third-class. Of all these, only nine women and girls and five boys, aged between fourteen years and nine months, were among the survivors. 1,514 people died altogether, making it one of the worst peacetime disasters in maritime history.

Among the other passengers on board were members of the West family from Bournemouth. The father was drowned, but his wife and infant daughters were rescued. The youngest, ten-month old Barbara, was later educated at Truro, where she eventually worked as a teacher. By then Barbara Dainton, when she died in 2007 aged 96, she was the last but one surviving passenger. She had always strictly maintained her privacy, and left a wish that her funeral, at the cathedral, should take place before any public announcement of her death was made.

HERE AND THERE, OR THEN AND NOW

Antony Payne, the seventeenth-century 'Cornish giant', reputedly stood 7ft 2in by the age of 21, and grew a further 2in after that. He was the son of a tenant farmer at Stratton, and during the Civil War he became a bodyguard for Charles I (who at less than 5ft tall was England's shortest-ever adult sovereign). Unlike several other giants in modern history, he apparently lived to a reasonable age. After he died at Stratton on the first floor of his house, the locals were unable to get his vast body through the doorway and down the stairs. They had to saw through the joists and lower him with ropes and pulleys. Relays of pallbearers were needed to take the massive coffin to the churchyard.

In 1600 the Willmott family bought a house at Bolhelland, near St Gluvias, built on a site where it was said bad luck always came to those who lived or stayed there. Three years later the son of the house left home to become a pirate, and returned home after making his fortune, but was horrified to see their once-proud house now neglected and decaying. Dodging creditors in the drive, he went to the back door, where his sister did not recognise him until he showed her a childhood scar which she remembered. They decided that for a joke she would introduce him to their parents as a traveller and friend of their son who had come asking for a room for the night, and then went to tell her husband about it. The son stayed at the house, telling his unsuspecting mother (who had also failed to realise who he was) of his exploits, and making no secret of his wealth. It suddenly occurred to her that if she did away with this stranger and stole everything he had with him, she could hide his body, sell his valuables and pay off their creditors. The daughter would be told that he had gone early to rejoin his ship at Falmouth. She then woke her husband, who had gone to bed, and they killed him. When their daughter returned next morning, they told her he had left. She said she had not thought he would leave so soon, as he had proved he was their long-lost son. Mr and Mrs Willmott were so overcome with remorse that they ran up to the room where they had left the body, and cut their throats. When their daughter wondered what they were doing and went to find them, she was so grief-stricken at what she saw that she collapsed and died.

The story, which may be true or may be legend, is mentioned in a pamphlet in the Bodleian Library, Oxford, *News from Penrin in Cornwall, 1618*. Bolhelland did exist, though it was a ruin by 1620 and the last remains were demolished in the mid-nineteenth century.

When Mary Kelynack, an 84-year-old former fish seller of Newlyn, heard about the Great Exhibition in London in 1851, she was determined to attend. Unable to afford such modes of travel as were available at the time, she walked the full 300-mile distance – in five weeks. On her arrival she was received by the Lord Mayor and presented to Queen Victoria and Prince Albert. She was granted free transport by train and coach back home, and lived with her happy memories for another four years.

In May 1908 Mary Duncan, a 60-year-old greengrocer of Helston, who had suffered from ill-health for some time, was found lying unconscious on the floor by her sister Susan. She sent for the doctor, who pronounced life extinct. He found that her false teeth were missing, and when he examined her, he discovered they were in her larynx. Death was due to suffocation, or as the papers put it, 'killed by false teeth'.

In November 1932, a man appeared before Truro Magistrates' Court on a charge of being drunk and disorderly at Truro eleven days earlier. Constable Bennetts had seen him reeling and shouting in the street, watched him fall down three times, and needed assistance to get him to the police station. He had two previous convictions, one at Penzance and one at West Penwith, and was fined £1. His name was James Etheridge Beer.

In November 1941, two neighbouring farmers near Camelford both claimed they were the rightful owner of Jenny, a particularly fine heifer. When the case came to court, the judge adjourned the case in court. Using the wisdom of Solomon, he led the farmers and Jenny to a nearby smallholding, where there were several cowmen employed by each, in separate groups. All the men were instructed to stand either side of the animal, and everyone watched as she ambled towards one particular cowman, nuzzled him, and gently put her front legs on his shoulders. The dispute was accordingly considered solved.

While she was on holiday in Newquay in the summer of 1946, Maisie Dunn from Essex allegedly made fashion history by being the first girl in Britain to follow the latest sensation from Paris, and wear a bikini in public on the beach.

In January 1960 the County pathologist Dr Denis Hocking learned that two elderly spinsters, the Sullivan sisters, Hannah, aged 85, and Mary, aged 94, had been found dead in their home in Gunnislake, a dwelling converted from stables, with an upper floor reached by a ladder. They were lying on the floor of the downstairs room. Mary had been dead for about a fortnight, her body thrown behind the door, and furniture placed over her, possibly a crude form of burial. Her head was badly bruised but there was no sign of bleeding, broken bones or brain damage. It was thought that they might have quarrelled, with Hannah hitting her sister over the head with a stool, thinking she was dead, and in her panic placing her under the furniture. Hannah presumably died later and was lying by the fireplace with her head in the ashes. Upstairs, in the bedroom with worn old blankets but no mattresses, the floor deep in rat and mouse droppings, were boxes full of pound notes, and deeds of property in Ireland. Some of the documents suggested that these ladies living in such squalid, poverty-stricken premises were distantly related to the Irish aristocracy. Hocking thought they probably died of general senile degeneration, accelerated by cold and exposure.

In February 1979, holidaymakers throughout the country were applying to book rooms at Pendennis Castle, which had apparently been turned into a hotel. It was being used as a youth hostel, and due to an error in a women's magazine it was mistakenly reported as being ideal for holiday accommodation. All this came as a severe disappointment to the couple who had asked for the bridal suite, and to the family from London who were planning to come in August and bathe on the ramparts.

In January 1988, churchmen and police feared that black magic was being practised by a few individuals who had stolen altar candles from a church in St Enodoc, and dumped black sheeps' heads on a farm at St Breock. Farmer Noel Warne was among those who concluded that somebody must have had a rather vivid imagination – or else thought it was a slow news day. Other theories suggested that the area had its own Beast of Bodmin or Exmoor at large – or that somebody must have run out of candles at Christmas.

In September 2005, the Cornwall Record Office, Truro, released a list of over a thousand unusual names which had been found in censuses and records relating to births, marriages and deaths, from the sixth century to the present day. It had been the idea of an archive researcher who had joined the office in 1999 and kept notes purely out of interest. Count yourself lucky that you never had the misfortune to be called any of these:

> Humfridus Hawkeye
> Boadicea Basher
> Abraham Thunderwolff
> Philadelphia Bunnyface
> Freke Dorothy Fluck Lane
> Foscurinus Turtluff Dyer
> Hephzibah Lillycrap
> Absolom Beaglehole
> Narcissus Backway

Moreover there were some remarkably appropriate pairings in the marriage registers, among them:

> 1636   Nicholas Bone – Priscilla Skin
> 1701   Hugh Hunny – Susanne Bear
> 1711   Charles Swine – Jane Ham

1791   John Mutton – Ann Veale
1802   Richard Dinner – Mary Cook

In 2010 Cornwall could claim to be the home county of Europe's most senior citizen, although he had recently moved. Stanley Lucas, a farmer, born at Morwenstow on 15 January 1900, moved to Marhamchurch as a boy. Owing to a heart condition he did not serve in either of the wars, but was a member of Bude Town Council from 1959 to 1970. For the last eleven months of his life, until his death on 21 June 2010 in London, at the age of 110 he was the oldest verified living man in Europe.

In August 2011, Rowe's Cornish Bakers, Falmouth, received an order for 700 Cornish pasties one day. The staff thought it must be a practical joke or a monumental error, until the manager convinced them it was genuine. Their munificent customer was actor Brad Pitt, who had come to film part of his new movie *World War Z* in the town and required the delicacies as lunch for his cast and crew.

On Christmas Day 2011, writer and comedian David Baddiel was among those taking part in the annual festive charity swim at Coverack Beach. Comedian Russell Brand, who was there to cheer him on, readily signed autographs and posed for photos with spectators.

Also by the same author

A Grim Almanac of Cornwall

Cornwall's Own

Cornish Murders (with Nicola Sly)

More Cornish Murders (with Nicola Sly)

West Country Murders (with Nicola Sly)